STRONG HAPPY FAMILY

UNEXPECTED ADVICE FROM AN IVY LEAGUE MOM OF TEN

To my parents John and Marion,
For whom there are no strangers,
Who taught me to love meaningful work
And to laugh at the days to come.

Front cover photo: Randee Gregg
Back cover photo: Prescott Baer

ISBN-13:978-0985872373
ISBN-10:0985872373

Let's Get Real Publishing
Chicago, Illinois

STRONG HAPPY FAMILY

UNEXPECTED ADVICE FROM AN IVY LEAGUE MOM OF TEN

Donna Baer

What people have said about Donna Baer:
(from the back cover)

Joe Biden: "You are a brave woman."
While he was a U.S. Senator, upon seeing the author herd eight of her small children through the streets of Washington D.C.

Larry King (weeping): "You've made me so happy."
At a parent-teacher conference, when Donna was teaching Larry's daughter at a boarding school in Maryland.

John F. Kennedy, Jr.: "Can you give me a ride?"
At Brown, when the author was working as the Campus Security shuttle bus driver.

George Steinbrenner: "Thanks for the beer."
At a summer night job during college, when Donna worked as a cashier at a liquor store in New Jersey.

John Malkovich: "That is a beautiful baby."
At Boston Market in Chicago's Lincoln Park. He was right, wasn't he, Trent?

Ray Romano: "Can I have my picture taken with you?"
At a cast party in Los Angeles. When Ray heard that there was someone in the room who had ten kids (a true novelty in LA), he wanted a photo.

Patricia Heaton: "I can't believe my friends from Chicago with ten kids just heard that!"
When Donna and her husband were Patty's guests at a charity event, after hearing Richard Lewis's raunchy routine. (The Baers were not offended.)

Dr. James Dobson: "I appreciated your warm words. You are a special lady and I enjoyed meeting you in Colorado Springs...I hope you sell a million copies."
This one is straight. Dr. Dobson wrote this after meeting with Donna in his radio studio in Colorado.

CONTENTS

Welcome to my Strong Happy Family

When I meet someone for the first time, I try to avoid mentioning that I have ten kids.

It's not that I'm ashamed of them, or that I fear ridicule— I really love my kids and our big boisterous life. I avoid mentioning the brood because it's a conversation stopper. Or at least it stops the part of the conversation that intrigues me. While I'm curious about my new acquaintance's family or work, all of a sudden I find myself answering questions about "the big life." My hunch is that new friends query me in order to sift out some advice that could help them in their scaled-back version of a Strong Happy Family. Though I would really love to hear *their* stories, I remember what it was like to be a young mother starving for parenting advice, so I usually wind up answering questions.

The questions I'm asked often huddle around certain themes. This book attempts to answer ten of the most frequent. They range from big-picture items (How do you get your kids to listen to you?) to the nuts and bolts (How do you keep them all fed?), and they are answered in no particular order. If you read this book and we ever get to sit down for coffee together, then we can talk about *your* life! I'd like that.

My story

I grew up just outside Manhattan, and attended Brown University when it was very trendy to do so. (I was there when John F. Kennedy, Jr., Bill Mondale and other glitterati graced the campus.) I met the love of my life at Brown, a strapping rugby player named Steve; we married, moved to Chicago, and became yuppies. I was made an officer in an investment-banking firm, and was poised to fall into a typical, high-achiever power-track career when I was blindsided. By a baby.

Now I don't mean that the pregnancy was unplanned and I struggled to find where the little creature would fit into my career plan. No, I mean I was completely caught off guard by how I fell head over heels in love with her. Twitterpated, dumbfounded, jaw on the floor. How could this happen to me? Suddenly, nothing mattered to me but caring for my baby, and making a wonderful home for the three of us.

When my maternity leave ended, I called my boss and said that I was not returning to work. My friends thought I was insane— that a few weeks of being home all day with a pre-verbal sack of demands would cure me of my ailment.

But just the opposite happened. The more I cared for my daughter, the more deeply I fell in love with her. The more I created amazing meals, the more I enjoyed cooking. The better I made our hip little apartment look, the more I appreciated—dare I say the word?— housekeeping! Despite my Ivy League education and my high-powered work experience, I was becoming the very thing I had once disparaged: a *homemaker*! And I had never been happier.

Then it dawned on me: if one child could create so much joy, what could two children do? My husband, who had fallen in love with our little girl too, and who was a major beneficiary of my discovering the lost arts of homemaking, agreed to test the hypothesis. We discovered that the joy to child ratio varied not geometrically but logarithmically!

Of course, to validate our test results we needed to repeat the experiment, so in the space of just three years we had three children. And while moving from "man-to-man" to a zone defense required adjustments, the test results were the same: more kids = more happiness.

My husband and I are the "all-in" types. We don't do things half-heartedly and we don't phone it in. What does a couple wired this way do with the test data I've described? We pulled the goalie for good. That was it. Bring them babies on!

And did they ever come! For over twenty years straight I was pregnant, nursing, or both. We received ten children in the course of two decades, two girls and eight boys. And we are a Strong Happy Family.

What I mean by "Strong Happy Family"

In my peculiar vernacular, "Strong Happy Family" does not mean that the kids don't argue (they do) or that I don't ever have down days (I do) or that the house is always picked up (it's not). What I mean by a Strong Happy Family is one in which each member behaves honorably, pursues interests heartily, and knows unquestioningly that he or she is loved deeply. A Strong Happy Family is not quiet, but it is peaceful. It is not sterile, but it is orderly. It is not silly, but it is funny. It's a place where kids are secure enough to go off the beaten track, but thoughtful enough to travel there without annoying others. A Strong Happy Family values ideas and people, not possessions and entertainment. And a Strong Happy Family can be any size.

If you are looking for ways to savor more peace and joy in your home, then you've come to the right place. Not everything in this book will be a "fit" for your family, but I hope that there will be something in it to lighten your load. This book is filled with seriously trench-tested principles that have kept a spring in my step and a smile on my face for over a quarter century of parenting. No ideas here written by childless "experts"; everything has been field tested repeatedly and should smack of authenticity, because it's all for real. Also, I'm not sharing a soft-focused recollection of what parenting was like: my tenth child is still in Kindergarten as I write this! When I reflect on the challenges of parenting, you will know that I am not looking backward through rose-colored glasses nor typing with French-manicured hands: I'm still in the boat with you doing the hard work of caring for a Strong Happy Family. And I am still happy.

Question #1:

HOW DO YOU GET CHILDREN TO DO WHAT YOU SAY?

Here is a conversation I have had many times:

> Haggard Mom: I could never have a big family—my life is already too chaotic. My kids just drive me crazy. They're always whining, they don't listen, they never pick up, they talk back, and they run me ragged.

> Me: How do you teach them to obey you?

> Haggard Mom: Obey me? What does that have to do with it? I don't know what you're talking about.

> Me: Don't you think if your children obeyed you, that your life would be more peaceful?

> Haggard Mom: I just hate that word: Obey!

"Obey" is today's four-letter-word, smacking of authoritarianism and conjuring the idea of abusive, dictatorial parents and drone-like children. It's perceived as anti-libertarian and classist. The mere mention of the word can play on a parent's insecurity and a child's natural rebellion. I understand; as a young parent, I was uncomfortable with the word myself.

You're not the boss of me

Part of our trouble with the "O-word" is that we struggle to find the basis for our authority. Just where do I, simply because I'm a parent, get off telling others what they ought to do? And why should I expect them to heed me? We are among the first generations to wrestle with this idea, because for centuries of Western Civilization there were accepted, authoritative guidelines for human interaction. Those guidelines were the basic social compact for all of Western society—secular and religious. They were encapsulated in the Ten Commandments, and right there, smack dab in the middle of the list was "Honor your father and mother."

When I first became a parent, I chafed at enforcing that rule. It wasn't that I doubted millennia of parenting tradition—clearly the rule had withstood the test of time. Goethe said, "He who cannot draw on three thousand years is living hand to mouth," and I had no disagreement. My problem was that I knew I wasn't really all that *worthy* of honor. I had done bad things, and thought bad thoughts, and not kept even my own standard of right and wrong. How in the world could I instruct my child to honor *me*?

But, I eventually realized that training my children to honor me was not for *my* benefit; rather, it was for theirs. Teaching children to respect authority keeps them safe and makes them happy. Obedient children don't play in the street, eat candy until they're sick, or walk around in a fog induced by refusing to go to bed on time. The most miserable child in the world is the one who despises his parents. He is also in grave danger.

Realizing that "it's not about me" gave me the confidence to do the hard work of child training, insisting that my kids honor my husband and me in their speech, actions, and even attitudes. We acknowledge regularly to our kids that we are not perfect, and that we often make mistakes. Nonetheless, our kids' duty is to honor us, because that's what's best for them.

Children love limits

Most children thrive where there are clearly defined expectations and boundaries. If a child is given no direction regarding meals or time management or language, he will most likely make choices that will result in his own unhappiness. Deep down, kids realize that they don't have the self-discipline or experience to make wise choices themselves, and they crave order imposed by a loving adult.

Often parents will institute wise standards for their family, only to be exasperated by a child who constantly tests the rules. They reason that the rules are faulty, or that the child is extraordinarily non-compliant, and so they abandon the standard. What that mom and dad don't understand is that their child longs for those rules, and even desperately wants them enforced. The child's apparent flaunting of authority was not necessarily a rejection of the laws, but likely a rational attempt to ascertain whether the laws are indeed in place. You can liken a feisty preschooler's testing his parents to a night watchman's checking to see if a door is locked. The watchman is glad—even relieved—to know that the door is locked, but he doesn't know that unless he tests the door.

When you make a rule or give a command that your child defies, celebrate! This is your opportunity to show your child that you do indeed love him enough to give him boundaries and to enforce them.

Discipline

Curiously, in our culture, if you exercise self-discipline you are admired as a virtuous person. If, however, you lovingly apply discipline to a child who cannot yet discipline himself, you are considered barbaric. Children depend upon loving parents to painstakingly teach them the rules for self-governance until they are ready to take over the job for themselves. A parent's thoughtful correction is his child's bridge between harmful chaos and self-imposed order. Without the bridge, children are marooned in destructive self-absorption. After the child crosses the bridge to self-discipline, parental discipline is no longer needed. A good parent will eventually work himself out of the bridge-building job.

For example, in our home, nobody has to tell mom and dad to go to bed at a reasonable hour. We know that we need a good night's rest to be healthy and productive, and we have the self-discipline to retire responsibly. Our ten-year-old, however, would stay up until he collapsed if he could. We impose on him a bedtime, and lovingly correct him if he resists it, because he hasn't yet disciplined himself. Since our seventeen-year-old has learned to self-regulate her sleep habits, we don't impose on her a bedtime. She has crossed that bridge.

Child training is not about behavior control

When you are focused on training your child to be obedient, it is very easy to concentrate on behavior, and to make behavior control the goal of your parenting. This is understandable, because bad behavior gets your attention—and it's really annoying. So it is tempting to "fix" the problem by controlling your child's actions.

This is very dangerous. For one thing, you run the risk of rearing a child who panders for approval, and puts on a show to look good when he knows there's an audience. When he is older, he will be called a hypocrite (and perhaps some other names that I won't list here). Your goal is not to control your child's behavior, but to help your child internalize wise standards. Anyone can control a sixteen-month-old, but if a sixteen-year-old has not developed self-discipline, you have lost the battle—and you may have lost your child.

A parenting paradigm shift

Consider this paradigm shift: My parenting goal is not to control my child's behavior, but to develop in him a virtuous soul. "Virtue" and "soul" are two words we don't think much about anymore, but they deserve a revisiting.

In the eighteenth century, "virtue" was a buzzword in the culture. The American Founders spoke of a "Republic of virtue," and Declaration signer Benjamin Rush said, "There can be no liberty without virtue." Integrity, prudence, diligence, justice, courage and restraint were prized attributes, and every citizen, be he farmer or Framer, valued them. A parent believed his utmost duty was to instill virtue in his child. Twenty-first century parenting goals of developing self-esteem, self-enjoyment, and self-actualization would have seemed absurd to a 1750's mom.

"Soul" is the other big idea that our culture has forgotten. Newspaper accounts of the 1912 *Titanic* disaster refer to the 1500 people who drowned as "souls lost." Back before we began to think of human beings as random accidental collections of matter, we thought of each individual as something more than the sum of his carbon-based molecules. There was something behind those eyes, within that bosom, that screamed transcendent significance. Any parent who gazes at his child's face knows this at his core. When you look into the wells of your baby's eyes, you see eternity. You know, despite what you might hear about humanity elsewhere, that your precious child is not just a pile of matter—he is a soul.

Shifting your thinking, then, from controlling a child's behavior to developing a virtuous soul can be life-changing, for both you and your child. Your consideration moves beyond the current annoying behavior to the virtue your son or daughter needs to cultivate. The issue is no longer "How can I make Sally stop lying?" but rather, "How do I train Sally to love truth?" Sally's lying is the red flag that alerts you to the fact that she doesn't yet possess the virtue of integrity. I won't choose to focus on removing the pesky flag; rather, the flag informs me where my daughter needs training in virtue.

Disciplining Sally to love truth is still going to take training. It is hard work. But if you do it consistently, Sally will eventually cross the bridge and possess the virtue of integrity. When she becomes a virtuous soul, she will no longer lie.

So just what does this kind of training look like?

How to train a virtuous soul

When a child is young, from about toddlerhood to age eight or ten, your focus is primarily on teaching him to obey his parents. The Bible, that age-old book of advice for sound living, has hundreds of wise sayings for adults, but really only one for children: "Children obey your parents." Obedience is the bedrock virtue upon which all the others must be built. A child must learn to obey his parents reflexively—without delay, complaint, or excuse. After his soul possesses the foundational virtue of obedience, all the other virtues can be put into place. (I talk about those virtues in the next chapter.) If you try to build an edifice of virtue without a foundation of obedience, watch out when the storms come!

Obeying without delay

We do not exit the womb with virtue. In fact, our inclinations are toward rebellion, self-aggrandizement, and deceit. Anyone who has raised a toddler knows this. If you tell an 18-month-old not to touch the electrical outlet, she will wait until she thinks you aren't looking—even checking to see if the coast is clear—then make a beeline toward the outlet. Did the little darling calculate that she had something to gain in her covert expedition? Hardly. She is just hardwired for disobedience.

As we train our children to be virtuous obeyers, their favorite tactic of rebellion is delay. If they can wear you down, they figure, they might just win. And sadly, I see this toddler trick work frequently. "Jimmy, come here. Jimmy, come here. Jimmy, I said, 'Come here.' Come on, Jimmy. You heard me. Come here... Oh never mind. I'll go get you." Or how many times have you heard, "I'll give you 'til the count of three..."?

To paraphrase Thurgood Marshall, "Obedience delayed is obedience denied." A child who does not obey his parents at once is a disobedient child. He has learned that he can manipulate his parents into at least compromising with him. If a child knows he has until the count of three (often with several fractions between two and three thrown in), he knows he has permission to disobey for a spell.

And the very worst part about allowing a child to delay his obedience is that it can make a parent angry. The longer a small child can hold a grown adult hostage, the more frustrated and angry the adult becomes. Finally, when the child capitulates, it is not because he has learned to choose obedience, but because he is terrified of his parent's anger. Both parent and child have become less virtuous.

I will speak more about the "Virtue Training Episode" in a moment, but for now, let me state clearly: We must never, *never*, discipline a child when we are angry and out of control. You run the risk of saying or doing something harmful to the child, and that is not how he is trained in virtue. Additionally, if you are angry, the episode turns from focusing on your child's virtue, to focusing on your flaws. If your child is pushing your buttons, and you feel anger welling up, tell your child to stay where he is, leave the room, and calm down.

Obeying without excuse

When children become verbal, they employ the obedience avoidance tactic of excuse:

> "Owen, please empty the garbage."

> "I just emptied it yesterday, and Liam never does it, and I was just sitting down to read a book, and the can hurts my fingers when I lift it."

Everything Owen just said may be true. But what is also true is that Owen is sitting on the couch when he should be emptying the trash. Clever children employ creative excuses for disobedience, and if you're not on your guard you might not even realize you're being defied.

If you want your children to become virtuous, you must teach them to obey without excuse. Owen needs to be taught that when he is given a command he is to rise, move immediately toward the chore, and say nothing but, "Yes, Mom" or "Yes, ma'am."

There are, of course, times when there is a reasonable argument to be made for non-compliance. The wise parent allows for this, but also instructs a child in how to respectfully request a reconsideration. This is what it should *not* look like:

> Mom: Tatum, empty the dishwasher, please.

> Tatum: I can't. Olivia's mother is picking me up for ballet in a few minutes.

Tatum should be trained to answer:

> Yes, Mom. (Tatum walks toward the dishwasher.) But may I ask you to reconsider? Olivia's mom is picking me up for ballet in a few minutes, and I want to stand by the door to watch for her so I don't keep her waiting. May I empty the

dishwasher after ballet?

Oh, so much better! Tatum has acknowledged that she ought to obey her mother right away, but she thinks she has information which, if her mother knew, might cause her mother to reconsider. Tatum presents the information respectfully, recognizing all the while that it is her duty to comply with her mother's request. Mom can evaluate the information and rescind the request if it seems reasonable. Mom has been honored; Tatum has been trained in virtue.

Obeying without complaint

One of the ugliest habits a child can develop is complaining. If a child does what he is instructed to do, but complains all the while, his soul—the object of our training—is not obeying:

> Dad: Fred, please put away all the toys in the yard.
>
> Fred: (Reluctantly picking up toys) It's not fair. I didn't even play with these toys. Nick never has to pick up. I hate this job. This is so stupid.

Fred's body might be going through the motions, but his soul is in frightful rebellion. Words are very powerful: As Fred complains, he is poisoning his own soul. He is persuading himself that he is entitled to his rebellion, and assuring himself that he is being cheated by being asked to submit to parental authority. For the sake of his own soul, Fred needs to shut up!

The Virtue Training Episode

Well, fine. Perhaps you've decided that, for the sake of her own soul, your child ought to obey without delay, excuse or complaint. But then she delays. Or makes excuses. Or complains. Or the trifecta: Complaining while making excuses while delaying. Now what?

Every child will test the rules (remember the night watchman), so you need to be ready with a plan of action. You need to be ready for a "Virtue Training Episode." As the word "episode" implies, this will require an investment of time. Virtue is not instilled by shouting, "Stop that," or by "whackin' 'em upside the head," as Madea would say. Have a seat. This will take some time.

Here is a typical "Virtue Training Episode" with a six-year-old. Let's look at it, and then analyze it.

> Mom: Peter. (She waits until she knows he hears her, and is looking at her. Then in a calm, conversation-volume voice she continues.) Please put away your Duplos.
>
> Peter: Not now. It's too hard. I hate cleaning. (Peter doesn't move.)
>
> Mom: (Dropping what she is doing and calmly moving right next to Peter, she looks him in the eye.) Son, I do not ask you to do things that are too hard for you. And we all must do things we don't enjoy at times. You have chosen disobedience. In the Ten Commandments, God tells you to obey me. When you disobey, your soul is in danger. To restore you to obedience, I must discipline you. I am going to spank your bottom three times. (She bends him over her knee, and spanks him exactly three times, then lifts him back up.)
>
> Peter: (He cries for a minute or two, then,) I'm sorry.
>
> Mom: What are you sorry about?
>
> Peter: I'm sorry I didn't pick up the Duplos when you told me. I'm sorry I disobeyed you.

Mom: I forgive you. Let's hug. (They hug until Peter lets go.)

Mom: Are you ready to obey now?

Peter: Yes, Mom. (Peter picks up his toys with a smile on his face, and Mom and Peter are sweet with each other.)

I know this sounds like it's made up, but it is a pretty accurate characterization of the type of episode that really happens. (There are many variations on the theme, of course, but I've shown you the prototype.)

Let's take a look at it step by step:

1. Mom makes sure that she has her son's attention by calling his name.

Sometimes parents begin barking orders at kids before they know they've captured their kids' attention; then the parents get frustrated because the kids don't comply. If a child is lost in a world of imagination, or intently focused on building something, it might take a moment to arrest his attention.

2. She waits until he looks at her.

Children need to be taught to look at their parents (and all adults) when they are spoken to. Parents need to remember to look a child in the eye too. Keep in mind, two souls are engaging in this episode, and the eye really is the window to the soul.

3. Mom speaks in a calm voice at normal volume.

Some parents yell orders at their kids; they train them to respond only to screaming. Teach your kids that you expect them to listen and comply when you speak in a normal, calm voice.

4. She makes a simple, clear command.

If Mom had said to Peter, "Straighten up this place," he would have been perplexed. Most kids don't see disorder the way we do and are at a loss to see the steps required to create order. Mom's simple, "Please pick up your Duplos," tells him exactly what she expects from him.

Sometimes when the kids are driving us crazy we say, "Stop it. Just stop it." Most kids can't figure out what "it" is, so they continue doing "it," thus making us more crazy. If you say, "Joseph, stop opening and shutting the cabinet," or "Marta, stopping hitting your fork on the table," you give them something to work with.

5. She uses the word "please."

Using the word please communicates respect to your child. Even though you are your child's authority, you acknowledge that this is a soul-to-soul episode, what Martin Buber might call an "I and Thou" moment. A child deserves dignity, even in the menial task of Duplo cleanup.

You are also modeling good manners to your children, and showing them how you hope they will treat their subordinates when they are older.

6. Peter plays the trifecta.

In eight short words, Peter delays, makes excuses and complains. He has disobeyed Mom's clear command and is not budging.

7. Mom reacts immediately.

Mom doesn't wait to see if Peter's delay will end if she begs. She does not fall into reasoning with him about his excuse. She does not become annoyed by his complaints. She drops what she is doing (very inconvenient at times, but worth it) and calmly walks over to Peter.

8. Mom quickly disabuses Peter of his excuses and complaints.

She quickly tells Peter what he already knows: that his excuses and complaints are invalid. She doesn't linger here, because his justifications are not the issue; they are a diversion. But she does let him know that he cannot hide behind his exculpatory construct; he must come face-to-face with his error.

9. In a normal conversational tone, Mom tells Peter what he has done wrong.

If Peter is to be disciplined, he needs to know exactly what he did wrong; otherwise, he might repeat his mistake. Peter was not being corrected because the room was messy; he was being disciplined for disobedience. If Mom wants to see him develop into an obedient son, he needs to clearly understand his error.

Mom continues to speak to Peter in a normal tone so he doesn't think he's being disciplined because she's angry. He needs to stay focused on the fact that he has disobeyed.

10. Mom appeals to transcendent authority.

"Obey me 'cause I said so" is an argument with a limited shelf life. Before a child is very old he realizes that mom and dad are not perfect, and that if their size or strength or wallet are all they have in their corner, maybe he doesn't really need to listen to them.

Mom reminds Peter that his duty to obey her—and her obligation to train him in obedience—come from someone greater than either of them. When a child obeys his parent, he is obeying his Creator. When he defies his parent, he is messing with God. Even a little child can understand the weightiness of that.

11. In a normal conversational tone, Mom tells Peter what the consequences of his actions are.

One thing that separates humans from animals is a human's ability to understand that actions have consequences. This feature of reason ennobles man. If you deprive a child of the just consequences of his actions, you are treating him as less than human. Though no person enjoys discipline, the very act of receiving a just punishment elevates us because it implies that we are rational beings.

Peter is not verbalizing these ideas to Mom, but at his core, he wants to be treated with the respect that only discipline will provide at this point. Mom tells him exactly what the discipline will be so that he understands that what is about happen is not a mercurial whim; rather, it is the just consequence of his free choice.

12. Without anger, Mom does exactly what she told him she would do.

When Mom does exactly what she says she will, Peter learns to trust her. Trust is crucial in the parent-child relationship, especially as the child journeys into adolescence. When parenting moves beyond nurturing the virtue of obedience into teaching other virtues such as prudence and courage, a strong bond of trust is the coin of the realm. (I'll talk more about that in the next chapter.)

Mom said three spankings. Peter gets three spankings. No more, no less. Her word is her bond.

13. She puts him over her knee to spank.

When a child bends over your knee to receive discipline, he understands that it is being administered within the context of love. You are cradling him as you dole out what will hurt you more than it will him.

Many parents cringe at the idea of spanking, preferring the use of time-outs to discipline their children. In my experience, time-outs often create a drawn-out diversion from correction. The child sitting alone in his room thinks only about escape (or the toys in his room), and rarely focuses on the mistake that earned him his punishment. A lovingly administered spanking focuses the mind, and creates the opportunity for dealing with the root of the youngster's problem.

14. Mom spanks only on the bottom.

A child's bottom is the perfect place to apply discipline. It is padded with fat and not heavily innervated. There is nothing a couple of careful swats could ever harm. When a child cries after a spanking on his bottom, it is more out of remorse than out of pain.

15. Mom gives Peter time to collect his thoughts and then to apologize.

After a loving spanking, a child needs a little time to process. The swat may sting, and the child may have to let out his sobs. When he is done, you need to wait for him to apologize. For a very young child, you may have to remind him to apologize; an older child will have learned that this is what you expect. By apologizing, your child acknowledges your authority, and admits his wrong.

16. Mom makes sure Peter knows what he is apologizing for.

Sometimes children will disingenuously apologize in order to be done with the episode. Other times, they might say they're sorry, but mean they're sorry they got caught, not sorry that they disobeyed. You should ask your child to repeat the charge so that you know his apology is sincere and that he admits his fault. If you detect insincerity or persisting defiance, you should linger and perhaps even repeat the spanking process.

17. Mom accepts Peter's apology.

I am surprised at how many times I hear adults say, "I'm sorry," only to receive no reply. When a child apologizes, he longs to hear you say that you've accepted his apology. Go ahead, say the words: "I forgive you." He needs to know that.

18. Mom offers a genuine sign of their reconciliation.

A child longs to be at peace with his parents. He wants to hear words of forgiveness, but he also wants to feel forgiveness. He wants to be hugged. You should never give a spanking without also giving a hug. Let your child dictate how long the hug will last; he is the one who needs to be reassured that he is forgiven and that you two are restored. You might be surprised to discover your strong, soulful hug will last minutes.

19. Mom gives Peter another opportunity to obey.

Nothing communicates reconciliation and mercy to a child like giving him the opportunity to make things right. After a child has come face to face with his error, has been corrected, has received his punishment and has been reconciled to his parents, he really longs for the chance to make things right. Do not deprive your child of that.

20. It's over.

Really. It's over. If you have forgiven him, then let it go. If you bring it up again you are communicating to your child that you haven't really forgiven him—that you were not truthful with him. You will violate his trust.

After a "Virtue Training Episode" a child is very sweet and tender. He is reveling in his restoration and grateful to know that his parents loved him enough to discipline him when he could not discipline himself. Don't spoil it by bringing up his fault.

Your child will disobey you again, perhaps even later on the same day. Then you will have to repeat the process. But for now, you and your child are at peace, and you have brought him one step closer to being self-disciplined.

Beyond obedience

It bears repeating: Obedience is the foundational virtue upon which all the others will build. Training a child to be obedient is tough, and it takes years. But if you are consistent, you will eventually work yourself out of the job of teaching your child to obey. You will have earned your child's respect and trust, and it will be time to build on your foundation. In those precious tween and teen years, you will be challenging your child to be courageous, diligent, prudent, self-less, truthful, merciful and wise.

In the meantime, stay the course! What enormous regrets you will have if, out of laziness or timidity, you abdicate the important responsibility of teaching your children to obey. Obedience is the foundation for all the other virtues, it is what is best for your kids, and it will make your home a peaceful haven.

Question #2:

HOW DO YOU RAISE HAPPY TEENS OR TWEENS?

This chapter builds upon the ideas introduced in Chapter 1; if your kids are still young, you may want to skip it for now. Or you may want to read it as a primer for the future!

As discussed in the last chapter, the bedrock virtue upon which all the other virtues rest is obedience. From the time your son or daughter is a toddler until the age of eight or ten, you'll want to focus on teaching your child how to obey you without delay, excuse or complaint. No child will ever perfectly obey, but if you teach him well, he will have a heart that is inclined toward obedience. Then you can begin to nurture other virtues in your child. If you try to develop derivative virtues before first teaching obedience, you will set yourself up for failure.

If you have taught your child obedience, then he will have a teachable spirit, and you are set to develop the other character virtues. You will, of course, introduce and elevate other virtues during the early years, but their development rests on a child who obediently accepts instruction.

Teaching the virtue of hard work (or diligence)

Our culture has become lethargic. Maybe it's from watching too much TV, or from eating too much, or from espousing hopeless outlooks that provide little inspiration for industry. I'm not sure why, but it seems as if much of the world has become just plain lazy. Laziness, both physical and intellectual, comes with its own punishments, making a person poor, unhealthy, bored, and boring.

A good parent will want to do everything in his power to buck this cultural trend, and teach his children the virtue of diligent, hard work. Children who are eager to roll up their sleeves and tackle the project at hand will become adults who are happy, fulfilled, and pursued in the job market.

Of course, it isn't just the culture we must buck in order to teach our kids to be industrious. We are all born with a little (or big) streak of laziness hardwired into us. Entropy (the tendency of systems to move to a state of disorder) is aided and abetted by our human nature. If you don't believe me, go peek at your kids' messy bedrooms. So, just how do we go about overcoming the culture and our human nature to nurture kids who love to work hard?

For starters, assign your children jobs. Even preschoolers who are still learning to obey can tackle small jobs: clearing the stairs, folding dish towels, emptying the flatware from the dishwasher. As kids get older, they can start to take on important chores to keep the home running: lawn mowing, laundry, house cleaning, window washing, minor repairs, meal preparation, babysitting, and elder care.

At first, they will do a terrible job, and they will do it slowly. You will rightly conclude that you could have done the whole job yourself thrice in the time it took you to explain, re-explain, inspect, correct, re-inspect, re-correct and acquiesce to the mediocrely completed task. But be patient. You're not teaching the art of vacuuming; you're developing the priceless virtue of diligence. Eventually, they will learn the job they've been assigned, and they will lighten your load. Eventually.

Furthermore, a child who has learned to contribute to the smooth functioning of the home through hard work will feel a certain amount of pride in his accomplishments. His contribution will strengthen his bond with the family, as he realizes that you depend on him as an integral part of your family's happiness and success.

Case in point: Our fourteen-year-old son Logan loves to work hard, and he took it upon himself to learn how to repair bikes. This is a highly valued skill in a home where most people depend on their bicycles for transportation to work and to sports. (Mom does not wear a chauffeur's cap in our family.) From garage sales and birthday gifts, Logan acquired a well-stocked toolbox, and from garbage bikes, he scavenged a supply of bicycle parts. Now, whenever a family member has a bicycle in need of repair, he goes straight to Logan, who adroitly does his magic. Logan's love of hard work earns him the gratitude and respect of the rest of his family. He is justifiably proud of the way he can serve the family, realizing that we truly value his skill and effort. His hard work has strengthened his bond with us. And he didn't have to take a self-esteem class to do it!

To be clear, Logan and all our children would be loved and cherished in our family even if they never fixed a bike, cleared a dish or made a bed. They are our children, and precious simply for the gifts that they are. I know severely handicapped children who will never be able to do a single household chore, yet are the light of their parents' lives. When kids contribute to the family by working hard, it's not in order to earn their parents' love; those labors benefit the kids themselves.

But just how did we inculcate Logan's love of hard work? Assigning jobs is easy, but teaching a child to love hard work is another story.

Basically, we try to instill a devotion to diligence primarily through these three means:

1) We model working happily.

My parents were excellent models to me for industry. They didn't just work hard; they enjoyed working hard. I can still picture my mom in her sweats blasting Bruce Springsteen as she sang and vigorously vacuumed the floor. My dad loved his workbench and tools almost as much as his Notre Dame football games. To them, work was, and still is in their retirement, a source of joy. As a child, I watched them, and actually looked forward to being able to own certain chores. It was big day in my life when I was given the privilege of ironing my dad's handkerchiefs. I guess Tom Sawyer had nothing on them, since they made work look so appealing!

When I had four kids all under the age of six, it occurred to me that I was working hard, but that I was communicating to my kids that my work was drudgery. I often complained or had a long face as I worked. I decided I would follow my parents' example, and choose to be joyful as I scrubbed the toilet or mopped the floor.

I knew I had mended my ways when we had a little visitor for lunch one day. As my son and his five-year-old friend finished their meal she asked, "Should we clear our plates?" My son replied with sincerity, "No. It makes my mom so happy to do work, we shouldn't take that away from her." My apparent love of work had almost bought me more of it! (Just to clarify: the Kindergarteners cleared the table that day.)

2) We don't pay allowance.

We have never paid our kids allowance. They understand that we all pitch in to make our family work, and it is our duty to serve one another this way. Some parents believe that they should give their kids allowance so that the kids can learn how to budget money. But until kids reach the age of ten or so, most of the work they do has no real value in the marketplace; we would be foisting an elaborate deception if we led our kids to believe that the market values a poorly-made bed, a half-swept floor, or a dog walked two hours late. Paying kids for work that isn't valued in the real world doesn't teach them how to budget; it teaches them how to freeload.

Furthermore, until a kid is about ten years old, he really doesn't have much of a need for spending money. We encourage our kids to learn to execute their chores well and to profit from the valuable on-the-job training they're receiving from their loving parents. They realize that once they've learned to work well under our guidance, they will have skills that will earn them money in the real world.

A curious thing happens just about the time our kids want to enter the marketplace as consumers: neighbors who have seen our boys doing yard work or our daughters taking the baby for a stroller ride call to hire our children! By the time he wants to purchase his first baseball card, a boy who has been trained to work hard at home will have been offered a job watering the neighbors' plants or caring for their pets. Once they've entered the marketplace, Adam Smith's Invisible Hand will motivate your children toward diligence. But if a child knows that he can choose between earning $10 for laboring under the hot sun weeding the neighbor's garden or being paid an allowance for merely existing, which do you think he'll choose consistently? An allowance tends to dissuade hard work.

When our daughters accept babysitting jobs, after they put the kids to bed, they clean up the house. Wouldn't you try to hire a sitter like that? The girls turn down more jobs than they can accept. When it snows, our boys wake up early to finish their school assignments (we home school, so they have some schedule flexibility), and start knocking on doors to find shoveling jobs. On a frigid morning, wouldn't that knock on the door be music to your ears? Since we don't automatically satisfy our kids' every material desire, they're more open to hard work.

I will now share with you one of our best teen raising tips:

3) We don't pay for anything!

That is, of course, a broad over-statement. We feed our teenagers, and give them lodging and pay their medical bills and buy their school supplies. On Christmas and birthdays we even buy them a few gifts. But when it comes to iPods and wardrobe and spending money and prom and camp, we have them foot the bill. This approach to teen finance has some lovely benefits.

First, it makes kids want to work, because they know they'll want to buy things. Moreover, they learn that to compete in the marketplace, they must work hard.

Second, cutting the purse strings makes our teenagers thoughtful consumers. If a teenager has put in eight hours on the lifeguard stand in order to bring home his $50, he thinks long and hard before plunking it down for a concert that will last two hours. If it's "other people's money" (OPM—sounds like opium), it's easy to get addicted to a spending lifestyle. Many young people get into trouble with debt because they've accustomed themselves to a lifestyle financed by someone else. Though your teenagers might pout about having to pay for summer camp, they will thank you later when they are debt-free adults.

Third, forcing a teenager to spend his own hard-earned money on entertainment means he doesn't take in so much entertainment. Instead of going out both nights of a weekend, he might work one night and play the other. Since much of what is offered up in the culture as entertainment is soul-rotting, limiting your teens' exposure to it is a good thing.

Finally, (and this is my favorite), if a teenager is spending fewer evenings a year on entertainment, and more evenings working, there are fewer times each year when you must say "no." Let's face it, teenagers throw a lot of mud against the wall to see what will stick:

"Can I go with eight other kids six hours away to an amusement park?"

"No."

"Can ten of us go camp on the beach?"

"No."

"Can I go all alone into the city to see a show?"

"No."

If kids are working hard to finance their own entertainment, they will propose fewer preposterous ideas for you to shoot down. You'll still have to say no sometimes, but you get to say it less. Less "no," less teenage consternated angst, more peace.

By refusing to pay for a teenager's discretionary purchases, you incent him to work hard. That hard work makes him value his time, value his money, value his reputation, and value his relationships. Realizing what it takes to make a living (or even to earn pocket money) makes him profoundly grateful to his parents for all they have done for him. "Grateful teenager" is not an oxymoron; it is the lovely consequence of allowing a teenager the privilege of working hard for what he values.

Teaching the virtue of honesty

We all value honesty. We want to trust and to be trusted. There really is no civil society unless there is trust. Yet many parents spin webs of lies before their children, and then wonder how it is that their children are not truthful. If parents wish to raise honest, trustworthy children, they must never lie to them.

The very first lie that many parents conspire to tell their children is one that sows seeds of distrust for years. Parents believe that it is innocuous—even endearing—and go to great lengths to perpetuate the ruse. When children learn that their parents have purposely deceived them from their earliest memories, they may feel profoundly betrayed. The lie is Santa Claus.

You might be appalled by my assertion. Many parents feel that Santa injects a harmless dose of fancy into a child's life. Some believe that you couldn't possibly raise a child without the Santa saga—that St. Nick is essential in creating the magic of childhood. Let me offer another perspective on the bearded fellow.

First of all, children don't need assistance incorporating fantasy into their lives. Dragons, pirates, fairy-tale princesses, magical wizards, and flying unicorns are already staples of their minds' narratives. In our home, we tell our children about Santa in the same context as we tell them about Pinocchio, Snow White and Harry Potter: they're all marvelous fictional characters whose stories delight us. Telling them the truth about Santa doesn't rob them of the magic of fantasy—it encourages them to embrace the whimsy of the tale. Since they have no plaguing intellectual reservations about the logic of the yarn, they throw themselves into it with abandon.

Secondly, in order to tell your children that Santa is true, you must conspire to lie to them—not just once or twice, but over and over again for years. You may not like my calling the story a lie, but truly, that's what it is. You must purposefully tell your kids things that are untrue, responding to their questions with answers that you know are wrong, and dismissing their honest attempts to make logical sense of the world. When your kids discover that you have lied to them, they will feel betrayed, suckered and embarrassed. You will have violated their trust, and you may not ever earn it back. Later, when you ask them to trust your advice about drugs or alcohol or premarital sex, you will have impeached yourself. As your teenager's hormones and peer group urge him to ignore your advice, his mind will scavenge his memory, looking for reasonable grounds for doubting your counsel. And there he will find, wrapped up with a bow, your primal deceit about Santa. "They've misled me before," he'll reason, "why should I believe them now?"

Another way that the Santa Lie strains the virtue of honesty is that to perpetuate it, you ask your enlightened children to become complicit in it. When a six-year-old learns that his parents have violated his trust, the first thing they ask of him is that he join in the lie. "Don't tell your little sister Santa isn't true. Just keep up the story so she'll believe it." What have they just asked of their child? Even though the realization of his parents' deceit has just disappointed him (perhaps even devastated him), they ask that he too become deceitful. Lying then becomes an accepted—even encouraged— behavior in the home. A six-year-old does not have the capacity to draw bright lines about when lying is good and encouraged, and when it is wicked and punishable. (I can't really see those bright lines myself.) Truth will become a relative thing in your home, something that, when useful is practiced, but can be subjugated for "important things"—like fairy tales. How can you correct your child for lying sometimes, and insist that he lie at other times? The cognitive dissonance will manifest itself in a low regard for the truth.

The final reason to discourage the Santa Lie is that it could easily diminish or preclude a child's faith in God. If a child learns that *his very first exercise in faith*—to believe his parents when they tell him about a generous, unseen person named Santa who displays attributes of omniscience and omnipresence—was a lie, why should he later believe his parents when they tell him about a generous, unseen person named God who is also omniscient and omnipresent? Fool me once, shame on you. Fool me twice...

If honesty is to be a prized virtue in your home, you must model it to your children from the very beginning. No white lies, half-truths or blatant deceit. Using your discretion, you might withhold information from children who are too tender to handle it, or who

31

are not entitled to it; but even then it's important not to tell lies. Let your word be your bond. Let your kids know that your yes means yes and your no means no. Then you will have the moral authority to correct them when they lie.

You will also have a cherished possession: their trust. This will prove to be the coin of the realm during their teen years. When you tell them, "Trust me. You do not want to go to that party," they actually will trust you.

Teaching the virtue of responsibility

Nothing can frustrate a parent like irresponsible kids. When kids lose their backpacks, leave their bikes out in the rain, or neglect their pets, we are justifiably perturbed. We expect them to care for what has been entrusted to them, and if they don't, they inconvenience us and cost us money. We want our kids to be responsible with their property.

I believe that the roots of irresponsible behavior can be traced to the strange law of the playroom, "You must share!" From the time a child is old enough to enjoy a playmate's company, he is instructed that he must, without question, share his possessions. What a strange thing this would be if we insisted that adults do the same! If one of my friends came over to my home and started trying on my dresses and looking over my cookware uninvited, I would feel a bit violated. But think about it: when a toddler comes to visit your home, he will make a beeline toward your child's most prized possessions, and start treating them like he owns them. When your child protests, you chide him, "You must share!"

Even though your child ostensibly owns his property, you deprive him of his property rights. You communicate to him that, although in theory he might own the Duplos, in actuality he has no control over how they are used. Your child soon learns that since he has no property rights, he is not responsible for the property. If you don't think that's true, tell me the last time you spent money changing the brake pads on your rental car. We don't take responsibility for things we don't own.

In our home, if a child owns a toy (or a bike or a skateboard), it is his to do with as he pleases. There are a number of toys at my home that are *mine*, and I choose to share those with visitors. But if my daughter doesn't trust her little guest with the Easy-bake oven that Grandmalynn gave her for her birthday, then I defer to her judgment. The oven is hers, she is responsible for it, and she gets to exercise full property rights. The net effect of this respect for ownership is that the oven is always clean and put away after a baking session.

There are times when sharing would be in a child's best interest, and he might be encouraged to consider that option. "Harrison, you might want to let Ike play with the basketball, because when you're at his house, you would like him to extend the same courtesy." Or, "Kent, it would demonstrate kindness if you let Nicky use your Play Doh now. He is a good friend, and I think it would mean a lot to him." Or, "Prescott, you know Annie's father is out of work. Even though you got those art supplies as a birthday gift, you could show compassion by letting her do something here that she can't do at home right now." There are lots of good reasons to share, and I like to remind my kids of them, but I never *force* them to share what is *theirs*, because that would mean a relinquishment of their property rights.

When kids grow up feeling responsible for the property they own, they learn to care for their possessions. As they get older, they become responsible for things much more valuable than possessions—people. You show me a responsible father who cares for the well being of his children, and I'll point you back to a boy who probably took good care of his lawn mower. Want to find a mother who responsibly watches over the affairs of her household? Look for the girl who cared conscientiously for her pets.

Other virtues

There are, of course, other virtues to cultivate in your children: courage, self-control, justice, and prudence, not to mention faith, hope and love. Perhaps I'll address those in another book. But if you are successful raising honest, responsible, hard-working kids, you might find that they develop those other virtues on their own, without much help from you.

Question #3:

WHAT DO YOU DO FOR STRUGGLING LEARNERS?

I homeschooled my ten kids—and from time to time, other people's kids as well. Consequently, I have striven quite intimately alongside a number of kids who struggled with "school." This is not an article about homeschooling per se; rather it's a description of strategies I developed to encourage kids who don't naturally succeed in academics. Some of these strategies are unconventional, and some are counterintuitive, but by employing them I have watched discouraged, unmotivated learners become curious students.

Timing is key

When I first realized that one of my sons was a struggling learner, my reaction was to push him harder. If it's difficult for him to read, well, we'll just drill phonics longer each day. If math facts don't come easily, I'll add supplemental math assignments.

Before long, I had turned my sweet little boy, who loved imaginary play and creating music, into a frustrated and cranky kid who had no self-confidence. Sensing what was happening to my son, our beloved piano teacher shared with me the story of her own son. "Your son reminds me a lot of my son Bob twenty-five years ago," she gently smiled as she recounted his story:

Bob was always a good boy, but never a good student. He had so much trouble that in high school he had to go to summer school every year, and only after several tries did he pass Algebra I. He didn't even bother applying to college, because he knew he'd never get in. Bob's dad had a friend who owned a factory, and offered Bob a job. He tried his best, but just couldn't master the skills it took to do most of the jobs in the factory. Finally, they put him at a station assembling cardboard boxes. All day, every day for a year, he put together boxes.

At the end of that year, Bob told us that he wanted to go to college. We were skeptical, but we didn't want to deny him the chance to go to college. We knew a man who was the dean of a small Bible college, and we asked him about taking a chance on our son's sketchy resume. The dean was a bit concerned, because at that particular Bible College, all freshmen had to take Ancient Greek. Despite this seemingly insurmountable obstacle, Bob enrolled in the college.

And something amazing happened. Bob began to excel at Greek and math! He recalls that there was something about the logic required in those courses that finally "clicked" in his brain—a brain that had had time in the factory to rest and mature. Bob finished his coursework at the Bible College, and then moved on to a state school to take more math. And to get a Master's degree. And a Ph.D.

Bob, who struggled to pass Algebra I in high school, is now chairman of the Engineering Department at a major east coast university.

Our piano teacher gave her son a precious gift: time. Time to mature and to let things "click." Time to let the cement harden.

It is so tempting to treat our kids like pre-programmed robots who are expected to march in lockstep with all other kids their age. Know your colors by three. Read by six. Do algebra by 13. Go to college at 18. Many kids are not designed to meet those milestones. It doesn't mean they're dumb; it means they have a different clock working. If you've ever tried to force a bloom on a plant, you know that you can make a plant flower earlier than it should, but the bloom is often sickly.

Bob's parents were not afraid to give their son's brain time to grow at its own pace. They were not caught up with what their neighbors might think about a son who worked in a factory, and they didn't push him to do things that he couldn't. They waited for him to bloom.

Every state has compulsory education laws, but it might surprise you to know that most states don't require Kindergarten attendance at all. In my state, school attendance is not required until age 8, and you have until the day before your 20th birthday to finish high school. If you are sensing that your 4 or 5 year old is not interested in letters or sounds, and doesn't like to sit still and focus, or could care less about coloring, *pause*. Why not give your child one or two more years of maturity before plowing into academics? It has been my experience that when a child is *ready* to read, it is almost effortless to teach him. I have had one child learn to read at age 4, and another at age 9! (The nine-year-old reader, by the way, is probably my most gifted child.)

Don't let your ego get in the way; you are not competing with your neighbors. You are guiding a precious soul who has his own unique gifts and rhythm. Take your foot off the gas and let time and space work its magic on your child.

Just say no to drugs

I know I may risk losing your indulgence on this one, but hear me out. Government schools are often financially incented to label kids ADD/ADHD and put them on behavior-controlling drugs. The more kids with labels, the more funding a school receives. Is it any wonder the number of learning disability diagnoses has skyrocketed in recent decades? Behaviors that we once called boyish or puerile or energetic are now called disorders. Fifty years ago, if a teacher couldn't manage the behavior of her classroom she was fired; today if a child cannot tolerate a dull, uninspiring teacher, *the child* is put on meds. If 10% of American children (and really, it's nearly 20% of American boys) must be drugged in order to endure a school day, does it not beg us to question our methods?

When I was at one of my class reunions at Brown, I got into a conversation with a Ph.D. who researched treatments for ADD/ADHD. I told him that I had one child who, though never diagnosed, seemed to exhibit the classic ADD/ADHD symptoms. I told him that I had resisted prescription treatments for him, and instead punctuated his school day with lots of exercise. Finish a math sheet—do ten pushups. Finish a phonics page—fifty sit-ups. Read for a half hour—run around the block. This expert in the field responded that his research indicated that what I had described was much more effective than any drug regimen; it just wasn't very feasible in a classroom situation.

But why not? Talk to your child's teacher, and ask her to consider introducing exercise into the curriculum. With all the pressure schools are under to improve students' fitness, it would seem like a reasonable request. And if your school is intransigent, consider your options. Don't make your child a captive of your local school's preferences.

Maybe there are indeed situations where medication is the best course of treatment for a young person. You are the best judge of your own child. I encourage you, though, to *diligently question* an education expert who believes she can't teach your kid without drugging him.

Ignore grades until high school

If you are reading this, you probably were a good student, and you no doubt cared a great deal about your grades. "A" stands for affirmed; "B" stands for bad person. I understand the value of good high school grades, but consider this for a moment: Short of complete failure, report card grades in elementary school mean *nothing*! Receiving a C in fourth grade Social Studies or a D in sixth grade math fixes nothing regarding a kid's academic career, job prospects or future happiness. Those grades are at best motivational tools; at worse they are cruel manipulative devices in an egotistical game of one-upmanship.

Think about it: a report card grade is the opinion of some 23-year-old, who may not share your family's values, as to how your child measures up to her notions of excellence in an extremely narrow band of skills. Pardon my French, but who the heck cares? Does she measure your child's emotional intelligence? His creativity? His mechanical aptitude? His perception with animals? His strength and agility? His courage? His patience? His logic? His character?

Yet many families treat those little report card scrawls as the validation of their parenting skills. They organize family time around getting good elementary school grades. They postpone family getaways because of science project deadlines, and hire tutors they can't afford to get that C up to a B-.

But I believe the worst thing that happens as a result of a family's grade-school grade obsession is the nightly torture routine called homework. If a struggling learner has just sat for seven hours being reminded of his inadequacies, the last thing he needs is to come home to the place that should be his sanctuary, only to have his parents reiterate his failures. A teacher has your child for his best seven hours each day, when his mind is fresh. At 3:00, it is time to put the books down and to use other parts of the brain and body. It's time to bake a cake, climb a tree, build a Lego, shoot some free throws, groom the dog, build a bookshelf, play the guitar, knit a scarf, paint a landscape, rehearse with your garage band, dig some worms, design jewelry, have tea with grandma, play catch with your brother, take apart a toaster, and do some chores. If drilling a few math facts or state capitals before bed will make your child feel more at ease about the next day, then go for it. But don't let the 23-year-old decide how your child will spend all his time.

Ten years ago, my friend Janey met with her academically frustrated son's fourth grade teacher to let her know that her son Andrew would do one-half hour of homework each night, and not a minute more. The teacher warned that Andrew might get zeroes on all his homework assignments, which might result in a "C" on his report card. The teacher was flummoxed when she discovered that her apocalyptic warning went unheeded, as Andrew and Janey stuck to their "half hour no más" guns. Andrew did go on to receive the scarlet letter "C" for the marking period. If you saw him now, a highly decorated Army Ranger who has scored at the very top of every assessment the United States Army has thrown at him, you would probably not sense that a "C" in fourth grade has hindered or emotionally scarred him. In fact, because his mother insisted that Andrew have discretionary time to think, explore and move, he was able to discover his true passions. (Janey—not her real name—is now a miracle-working Wilson-certified tutor. Contact me at my website stronghappyfamily.org if you'd like to reach her.)

Make sure your child is excelling in something

No matter how much your child struggles in school, trust me, he is good at something. Einstein said, "Everyone is a genius. But if you judge a fish on its ability to climb a tree, it will live its whole life believing that it is stupid." Your job as a parent is to discover your child's "genius," and do whatever you can to let him earn success there. Notice, I said *earn* success. Struggling children are very perceptive when it comes to phony praise, rigged results and the "everyone gets a trophy club," and they resent being patronized. You need to help your child find something he loves and let him *work* at it. It might mean investing in some tools, or a musical instrument, or sports equipment. It could involve stocking an art shelf, a baker's cabinet or a sewing kit. If your child has experienced some failure, he'll need gentle persuasion to take a risk on something new. Don't berate him if it takes him a while to light on something that delights him. You want to focus on his earning success. And the confidence that he'll gain from his first success will encourage him to branch out and try even more new things. Who knows, he might even circle back with his newly earned confidence and become an excellent student.

Don't worry if your child has a hobby or interest for only a season. By adult measures of time, a year is a passing fancy. For kids, twelve months is an enormous fraction of their childhood or adolescence. At times, an intense year of exploration is all a child needs from a particular interest. He harvests from the activity what it can give him, then hungrily moves on to another field.

As parents, we sometimes force a child to stick with an activity long after his interest has waned, simply because we've invested money in dance shoes, a lacrosse stick or a cello. But truthfully, do we really think our kids are going to become professional dancers, lacrosse players or cellists? Probably not. We know that the activity is time-limited and serves a certain developmental function in childhood. Kids know this too, and are very good at indicating to us when they have fully harvested a field. Since the kids are the ones laboring in those vineyards, we should listen to them carefully. When only the corners of the field are left to glean, it is time to move on!

Unplug

Most young people are inexorably drawn to technology, but struggling learners often retreat into the digital world as a refuge from failure. Gaming is a distraction that offers a counterfeit of the success your child is craving. "Black Ops" might provide a buzz, but every child knows that a victory on Xbox has no intrinsic value—it will not build skills, nor will it boost confidence.

A struggling learner needs to be lured away from (or banned from!) the screen. Depending on your child's attachment to the machine, this might take some intestinal fortitude on your part. If you feel you must permit some screen time in your child's day, ration his doses carefully. In our home the gifted and the struggling alike are permitted to game only on Friday nights and Saturday mornings. By lunchtime on Saturday, they have had their fill of exploding aliens and don't pester me about video games during the school week.

Remind yourself, if you feel your resolve regarding screen bans weakening, that every minute your child spends gaming is a minute that he does not spend earning success. If all things high-tech seem to be his delight, then try to steer him toward programming or web design or some other tech hobby that has real-world value.

Unplugging would also include removing those darling auricular appendages called earbuds. Strugglers can easily become introverted, slipping into a solipsistic narrative with its own private soundtrack. Disconnect the white cord, and connect with your child, who is craving encouragement and relationship with a person who doesn't berate him for being slow. That might mean that you have to listen to his music with him on speakers, but hey—you went through labor for him, you could probably endure dub-step music.

Create a peaceful space for study

By the time your child reaches the teen years, he will need a quiet place for study or work. Creating a peaceful nook, much less a peaceful home, requires intentional design. But you *can* create peace, and that is what a late bloomer craves. Every little space that can harbor distraction will be one more battle your child will have to engage in order to concentrate.

If at all possible, find your teen a corner of a room (literally a corner) where you can place a desk or card table. A corner cuts way down on distracting sights. Forget about using an office chair; those wheels and swivels and hydraulic levers introduce too much commotion. My concentration chair of choice is the wing chair—it is comfortable, it doesn't move easily, it promotes attentive posture, and it wraps around at head level, eliminating visual distractions.

And do I need to mention that his phone needs to be docked in a different room—out of earshot? The little ping of a newly delivered text message is enough to throw any teenager into a full gallop. Keep the world at bay for a spell as your child toils at connecting the dots of the universe in his head.

Give your child big ideas to think about

"Good students" are often the ones who color neatly within the lines, and turn in the assignment early, even if they know it's busywork. The correlation between effort expended and knowledge acquired is irrelevant to them. They sometimes miss the forest for the trees, memorizing how to perfectly execute a problem without understanding what that solved problem tells you about the world. "Bad students" often have contempt for that approach to learning.

Many kids who perform poorly in school are actually very bright. They could easily execute the work they are assigned, but refuse to because they don't perceive the assignment's significance. In a way, this is a very mature approach to work. If you can't convince me that an investment of my time is worthwhile—that it has a real world application—I will eschew it. Give your student a reason to work hard in school by filling his life with the big ideas that require effort to explore. These engaging thoughts connect schoolwork to life.

Giving your child big ideas to ponder makes him crave the tools necessary to explore those ideas. When your children are young, introduce big ideas through the biographies of people who lived admirable lives. Every struggling learner needs to read or hear the biographies of Thomas Edison and Albert Einstein, two boys who were labeled learning disabled. Larger-than-life heroes inspire kids to persevere and be courageous. They model problem solving, creative thinking and risk taking. If your child can't yet read great biographies by himself, read to him; you might get inspired yourself. And the very act of reading great literature to your child informs him that books can be interesting—just the motivation he might need to take his phonics homework seriously. (Check my website, stronghappyfamily.org, for a list of great literature for children.)

In high school, talk about big ideas with your kids: Political philosophy. Keynesian and Austrian economics. Darwinism and Intelligent Design. The Middle East. Calvinism and Arminianism. String Theory. God. Share with your teenager whatever big ideas interest you. Even if he doesn't follow you perfectly, you've informed him that there are wonderful things to ponder, and that the tools he's acquiring in high school actually do have a meaningful application. Big ideas also pull a teenager out of the self-absorbed ego maelstrom that is adolescence.

Praise something everyday

When you tussle with a discouraged student, it is easy to see only faults. Part of a parent's job *is* to identify and correct flaws for a child. It is easy though, to go into correction mode and get stuck there. You must discipline yourself to daily find praiseworthy things your child has done. I know, some children make this easier to do than others, but all children do something that merits commendation. "I like the way you arranged your dresser top." "What a great outfit you put together!" "You make the best peanut butter sandwiches." "I love that song you played on the piano." Plumb the depths of your mind—there's a compliment lurking there.

Whenever possible, lead with a word of affirmation. Untold grief can be avoided if a reprimand about neglecting the garbage chore begins with an acknowledgment of how great the swept floor looks. If you need to discuss the sensitive topic of academic achievement, begin with highlighting success. A child who knows that his efforts have been appreciated is inclined to receive lovingly offered advice. If you indicate to a kid that no matter how hard he's tried, all you can see are his faults, he will shut you out quickly. In the book of Proverbs it says, "A word aptly spoken is like apples of gold in settings of silver."

Don't be discouraged if your child struggles to learn. Your discouragement will be contagious! Realize that your kid is growing at his own pace, and learning in his own style. Adjust your expectations, correct your parenting, fill your mouth with praise, and enjoy the unique kid who is just passing through your home. When he's the department chair at his university, he'll send you flowers.

Question #4:

HOW DO YOU KEEP THEM ALL FED?

This is probably the question I am asked most frequently. For some reason, of all the jobs associated with raising a big family, the task of feeding them seems most daunting to the casual observer.

While regularly feeding a big crew is not effortless, there are several secrets that make it totally doable for even a kitchen klutz. What's more, these tricks can also be put to use for a family of two or three or four, streamlining meal production and redeeming precious time for other family activities.

I've boiled (pardon the pun) these secrets down to nine principles that I use every day to feed my dozen:

1. Choose the right equipment.

I confess I drool a little bit when the Williams Sonoma catalogue arrives. I love copper lined pots and stainless steel gadgets and specialty bakeware. But my kitchen cabinets and drawers demonstrate cookware restraint. Once a year, I go through every drawer and cupboard and ruthlessly evict every article that has not paid its rent. In other words, if I don't use it regularly, out it goes. I keep some steel shelves in the basement for those items that get occasional use but only deserve off-site housing. The result is maneuverability. Items are easily accessed, everyday wares are at my fingertips, and drawers open and close effortlessly.

When choosing which items get a lease renewal, I always bias toward large—as large as will fit in my cabinet. There's nothing you can make in a one-quart pot that you couldn't make in a six-quart pot, and it takes the same amount of time to clean each. (Don't waste your time putting pots and pans in the dishwasher—they never really get clean, and you waste the space you could have used for plates.)

Here is the list of cookware items that have been excellent long-term tenants in my kitchen:

- Two steel 14-inch mixing bowls (great for quadruple batches of cookies, enormous salads, marinating 12 pounds of chicken or whipping up merengue)
- One heavy-duty plastic bowl (the biggest that will fit in my microwave)
- One 18-inch non-stick skillet (also good for walloping intruders)
- One 12-inch non-stick skillet (stick skillets are for people with leisure time)
- One 16-quart pot (4 pounds of pasta—no problem!)
- One 12-quart pot (you might need 6 pounds of ground beef to go with your pasta)
- One 8-quart non-stick pot (because life wouldn't be the same without alfredo sauce)
- Three 18x12-baking pans. Twenty pounds of short ribs—check. Three Christmas lasagnas— check. Quadruple batch of brownies in one pan— check.
- Six large cookie sheets. Bake all six of those frozen pizzas at the same time. Or make a dozen dozen cookies in an hour. They also make great trays for hauling meat to the barbecue grill.
- One enormous colander, stored right under the sink. (To find out

why you want an enormous one, see my "Macaroni and Cheese that is not Just for Preschoolers" recipe on my website, stronghappyfamily.org.)

- Twice as many slotted spoons, spatulas, tongs, mixing spoons, whisks, and excellent knives as you think you need. (Nothing is more annoying than stopping in the middle of a masterpiece to scrub down a spatula.)
- One Kitchenaid mixer. Mine is a 5 quart. I wish I had a bigger mixer, but the one I have can still prepare two cakes at a time. Speaking of cakes, don't miss the easy chocolate, chocolate cake recipe (voted "Best Cake Ever" by my son's college dorm) on the website. Mmmmm.
- Four Bundt pans—'cause when you make the best cake ever, you're going to need lots. And you'll want to have a couple of cakes on hand in the freezer for sick neighbors. Nothing nurses a body back to health like chocolate cake.

Some other items that get frequent use in my kitchen are

- Three electric waffle irons, all different kinds. On a lazy Saturday, I like to make giant bowlful of batter, and then let the kids make their own waffles as they emerge from their slumbers.
- One food processor. When I bother taking it out, I make it earn its spot on the counter by shredding, slicing or dicing several different foods.

2. Keep a fabulous pantry.

I know. That sounds so "Little House on the Prairie." But keeping lots of really fine dry goods on hand means there's always something tasty for dinner, even if you haven't been to the market for a while. I buy most of my pantry at Wal-Mart or Trader Joe's, usually a dozen of each at a time. (For economy, another great place to shop is Aldi.) While every family has its own palate, here are the tried and true staples that I stock:

- Stock. (I thought it would be cute to start with that.) Those big resealable quarts are my favorite.
- Pasta, pasta, pasta. Every shape, every size. If you don't like my pasta, you're probably an alien.
- Rice. Basmati and Thai seem the most versatile. I love brown and wild, but they don't sell well with the young crowd around here.
- A big hunk of Parmesan cheese. It adds savor even if the recipe isn't Italian.
- Panko bread crumbs. Don't even waste my time with crumby regular crumbs.
- Grape jelly. (Don't ask why. OK, see the meatloaf recipe on the website.)
- Soy sauce. Kikkoman.
- Oil. Extra virgin olive oil for when it's a breakthrough ingredient. Regular olive oil for when it's not. Canola oil for baking and deep-frying. (Come on, you have to deep fry every once in a while!)
- Nuts: Pinenuts, walnuts, cashews, almonds, pistachios.
- Dried fruit: Apricots, blueberries, and craisins.
- Beans: Black, garbanzo, pinto.
- Canned goods: Crushed tomatoes, diced tomatoes, olives, corn, and clams. Always rinse and drain them in very cold water, and no one will ever know they're not fresh.
- Trader Joe's Seven Grains. I've served these over and over at dinner parties, and am always embarrassed when asked for the recipe. Here it is: Add package of grains to boiling water.
- Oatmeal. You'll see why if you try my homemade granola recipe found on the website.
- Honey.
- Chocolate chips.
- Pancake mix.

- Chocolate cake mix.
- Brownie mix.
- Seasonings and herbs. Some offbeat, inexpensive blends I've discovered are Cavender's All Purpose Greek Seasoning, Goya Sazonador Total, and Tony Chachere's Original Creole Seasoning.
- Flour, sugar, baking powder, baking soda, cornstarch. Boring, I know, but essential.

3. Keep a full freezer.

If you don't own a stand-alone freezer, get on Craigslist. Having the mothership tucked in the basement or garage lets you take advantage of great sales on meat (and ice cream, of course), and lets you store those precious leftovers.

Some of the best deals on meat are also those intimidating foods: turkey, pork roast, pot roast, whole chickens. Have no fear, they can be very simple to prepare. You can, for all of the aforementioned meats, simply bake for several hours, and you'll have a crowd pleaser. Add some finesse and you'll be crowned queen. (See my website recipe section for regal finesse instructions.)

You should, of course, have some good cuts on hand that don't require several hours of baking, because a long lead time doesn't always square with your schedule. Boneless chicken breasts, pork fillets, salmon, tilapia, shrimp and tenderized rib-eye steaks are often reasonably priced and can flex with your mood. (I'll put some of my favorite quick concoctions for these cuts in the website's recipe section too.)

And let's not kid ourselves. You need to have frozen pizza. I never understand why pizza gets labeled junk food. Tomatoes, cheese, bread, vegetables, meat, garlic: the ingredients for 75% of my favorite Italian restaurant menu items. In our house, Friday night is frozen pizza night for the kids. (It's date night for the husband and me.) A ten-year-old can prepare a frozen pizza dinner, start to finish—including cleanup—all by himself. And he should—you deserve a night off.

4. The chef invests her time into just one meal a day.

In our home, dinner is a time to connect; people tend to gather and want to touch base. Consequently, dinner is the meal where I focus my efforts.

Curiously, family members do get hungry at other times of the day. Breakfasts and lunches on normal weekdays are somewhat laissez faire affairs, largely due to our non-converging schedules. I keep the cabinets stocked with cold cereal (including homemade granola) and a variety of breads and peanut butter, and the refrigerator is full of cold cuts, eggs, cheese, fruit and milk. And here's the rule: if you go to the kitchen to create a sandwich or an omelet, or to warm up leftovers, you have to offer also to make one for anyone within earshot. That way, bigger siblings care for little ones, develop rudimentary kitchen skills, and learn to think about the needs of others. (That's a great life skill to work on, especially in the teen years.) Spreading the workload for the first two meals of the day conserves my energy and creativity for dinner. It also gives picky eaters control over more of their food life. Nothing says empowerment like heaping peanut butter on white bread.

If someone needs to pack a lunch to go, that is his own gig. A seven or eight year old can put together a wholesome bag lunch. (Remembering to put it in his backpack is a whole other thing.)

I've found that my family doesn't mind simple routine breakfasts and lunches if I can keep them guessing for dinner.

5. Think ahead.

I don't mean a month ahead, or even a week ahead. I've tried planning menus out like that, and I hated it. It was so constraining! Besides, I can never tell a month in advance if the rugby team will be joining us for dinner, or if there'll be a sale on fresh salmon. Further, those month-in-advance cooking plans generally feature casseroles. Frozen casseroles. Every time you inextricably intertwine two ingredients, you double the chance that one of your eaters will reject it. Make a 6-ingredient casserole, and you might as well also order take-out.

When I say plan ahead, I mean plan eight hours ahead. Decide at breakfast time what you'll serve for dinner. Then, take your meat out of the freezer, or crank up the crock-pot, or budget time to stop at the market. Deciding at 8 a.m. what's in store for 6 p.m. takes lots of stress out of 5 p.m. (commonly known as the witching hour, when all babies cry, all toddlers are cranky, all grade-schoolers are bored, and all teenagers are impatient. Well, almost all.)

6. Enlist help— but not too much help.

Creating an appetizing, healthful meal for any size group is a production. Doing it seven days a week is a jail sentence, unless you are strategic about enlisting help from the inmates. I assign one child at a time to help me with meal preparation and table setting. More than one helper usually gets in the way.

Delegating tasks requires a bit of organization (and often a lot of patience), but it can really lighten the load. The longer an apprentice works with you, the more culinary skills he'll acquire. Eventually, you can work yourself out of a job. And your future sons-in-law and daughters-in-law will shower you with thanks. (That's begun to happen to me. It's sweet!)

I usually start my apprentices off with table setting. Forks on the left, knives on the right, etc. That can test the limits of Kindergarteners, but eventually they can move on to salads, sauces and sides. Perhaps the biggest benefit of this indentured servitude is the time it creates for thoughtful, relationship-building conversation. With the right approach, a discussion that begins with whether to add cucumber to the salad can end with your child's frustration with the bully on the baseball team.

7. Keep the picky eaters at the dinner table by isolating components.

It is nearly impossible, in a family of any size, to create a meal that *everyone* will enjoy. At almost every meal I disappoint someone. I try to respect the fact that we all have different palates, and that little ones have very parochial tastes, but as my mother from Brooklyn would say, "I am not a short order cook." There is one and only one meal on the menu each evening (call it *prix fixe*).

To minimize the trauma, I try to make a dinner composed of a few separate components, which may—or may not— be combined. Buttered pasta in one bowl, some broccoli in another and a savory shrimp and garlic broth in a third: Mix and match as desired. Or perhaps a bowl of Thai sticky rice, a separate tray of sautéed sliced chicken, a pot of steamed vegetables, a can of cashews, and a jar of plum sauce: You could created a dozen combinations with those components. Imagine all the meat and potatoes permutations you could create. Picky eaters can pick what they like, while not sentencing the adventurous eaters to a diet of dull.

8. Make enough to have leftovers.

Whether you make two pounds of pasta or four, the time investment is the same. Even if my dinner headcount is small, I still cook for a crowd, in order to enjoy the luxury of leftovers. This can be a lifesaver when your sons reach the age when they require "second dinner," (Age: 14, Time: 9 p.m.), or when the baseball game's extra innings stretch right into dinner prep time.

My storage container of choice is a Zip-lock bag, adorned with a Sharpied label. I have one dedicated shelf in the fridge, right at eye-level, reserved exclusively for leftovers, so everyone knows where to look for them. Since leftovers are right at eye-level, I am visually reminded to use them up. The Zip-locked contents can conform to the available space, and I don't have to use up a whole kitchen cabinet just to store empty plastic containers.

9. Have everyone chip in for cleanup.

Everyone loves to eat; no one likes to clean up. It's a law of nature. But if everyone chips in for the clean up, then it doesn't have to be drudgery. Crank up the tunes and make it a party. I ask each person, when he rises from the table, to make two trips to the dishwasher. That alone takes care of clearing most of the table. Then, I put one person on storing leftovers, one on washing pots and pans (we let time dry them), one person wiping down counters and another sweeping the floor. I come along and fill in the gaps. With this approach, even a feast can be put away in fifteen minutes. And we've had some amusing sing-alongs in the process.

Feeding your crowd on a daily basis is not a no-brainer. It requires a good active brain, but you have that. (If you didn't you wouldn't be investing your time trying to improve the quality of your family's life.) Put those brain cells to work creating delicious meals that will draw your family together, keep them healthy, and make them look forward to being home.

Question #5:

HOW DO YOU HANDLE THE HOLIDAYS?

Creating holiday memories

We all have cherished family memories that connect us with the past. Just the smell of onions and celery sautéing takes me back to Thanksgiving mornings of my childhood, watching my dad create his celebrated turkey stuffing. Traditions are important because they connect a family in a bond of shared experience. Like developing a team identity, creating a culture of tradition unifies a family.

The onerous day-to-day demands of caring for a family, however, can make the proposition of establishing family traditions daunting. If I'm struggling just to nurse the baby and feed the toddler, how in the world am I supposed to "Norman Rockwellerize" my home? The secret, I've found, is to choose a few great annual touchstones, and do your best to keep those up. Kids will remember those landmarks into adulthood, and will cherish the memories they evoke even after they've moved away. Traditions are a way to continue loving your child even after you've died.

The following are a few ideas that have worked well in our home. Maybe a peak at our family traditions will help you invent some doable ones of your own.

Food, food, food

Almost all of our holidays have menu items associated with them. Christmas Eve: linguini in clam sauce. Christmas Day: lasagna. Independence Day: mango chicken flatbreads to go. St. Patrick's Day: corned beef, carrots, cabbage, Manny's Irish soda bread, and green milk (or beer). Thanksgiving: turkey with all the fixings (big surprise). April Fool's Day: meatloaf baked in individual muffin tins, topped with pastel-dyed mashed potatoes. (They look like adorable cupcakes. April Fool!) And of course, there are more. (I've listed a few of these recipes in the next chapter of this book, and at stronghappyfamily.org.)

I try to keep those recipes sacrosanct for the holiday, so that they hold a special place in the kids' memories. I figure, I'll have to feed the family on those days anyway; why not create a special, easily executed menu, the smells and tastes of which will lock in a tender recollection? Scientists tell us that memories evoked by smells and tastes are the most poignant because they are stored in the brain at the molecular level. Think about it: those savory molecules might one day remind your child that he is cherished! Long after you're gone, those warm memories, triggered by olfactory nerves, might be just what he needs to get him through a crisis. We can powerfully love our children by cooking up great holidays.

None of my holiday menus require advanced culinary skill, and none call for exotic, expensive ingredients. I searched to find menus that are highly replicable. Pulling off a holiday meal means planning in advance, but it shouldn't require traveling to foreign ports or breaking the bank. In my recipe file I keep a shopping list for each special supper. A few days before the holiday, I pull out the card and let it guide me through the grocery store. (I've begun transferring those cards to notes on my iPhone.) Using those lists frees up my brain's memory bytes for other useful storage and ensures that I'm not making a mad dash to the 7-Eleven on Thanksgiving morning.

If all you've done to create family memories is developed a few, simple menus, you've done well. Don't burden yourself by adding more traditions if these cause stress. But, if you want to slowly slip in some other traditions, here arc a few ideas that have worked well in our home.

Read something

Having something that the family reads aloud or recites on each holiday can build beautiful, content-rich memories. You can communicate to your kids that your traditions are not just about warm fuzzies, but that your family celebrates big, transcendent ideas. Repeatedly connecting your kids to the stream of Western Civilization and to great thinkers of the past elevates them and helps them to understand that they are part of something much bigger than themselves—they are not only beloved parts of your family, they are important members of society.

Here are some things we have read on holidays:

Fourth of July: *The Preamble to the Declaration of Independence.* (We actually make our kids memorize this.) In the nineteenth century, American Independence Day celebrations included a group recitation of the whole Declaration, including all the grievances! Hearing the words that inspired our Founders to pledge their lives, their fortunes and their sacred honor engenders gratitude in a child (and in an adult).

Thanksgiving: *Psalm 95.* It's funny how in late November, many people talk about being thankful, without ever mentioning just to *Whom* they are thankful! It's kind of weird to say thanks to no one. For over two hundred years in America, Thanksgiving was a day set aside to give thanks to our Creator, and it really is a fine tradition. Children who are reminded to thank God for what they have are less prone to feel entitled to "stuff" or to be arrogant about their talents. Acknowledging that all we are and have comes from God inculcates the lovely virtue of humility.

Memorial Day: *America the Beautiful.* (all the verses, sung if you can!) The first verses of our patriotic standards are often very familiar. But many of the later verses are also filled with ennobling lyrics that elevate the spirit and inspire virtue:

> *O beautiful for heroes proved*
> *In liberating strife,*
> *Who more than self their country loved,*
> *And mercy more than life!*
> *America! America! May God thy gold refine*
> *Till all success be nobleness,*
> *And ev'ry gain divine!*

Passover: *Exodus 14.* Passover is the longest continuously celebrated religious holiday in human history. Its theme of freedom from slavery echoes throughout history, inspiring countless liberation movements including the Emancipation of American slaves in the 1860's and the Civil Rights Movement of the 1960's. And related to that is...

Easter: *John 20.* You won't find a bunny or a chocolate egg in the whole story, but you will read what many people consider the pivotal event in all of history. (I wrote a book for teens, tweens and their parents discussing Passover and Easter. It's listed under the "Resources" tab on my website stronghappyfamily.org.)

Christmas: *Luke 2.* Even if you're not observant, a love of cultural literacy should compel you to read this to your kids. If your kids grow up thinking that Christmas is Santa's birthday, they'll be cut off from two thousand years of Western Civilization. Luke 2 tells a beautiful story, especially in the old King James Version, and your kids need to know it.

Valentine's Day: *Shakespeare's Sonnet XXIX.* OK, Valentine's Day is not a touchstone of human civilization holiday; but it is so much fun. See if some of your kids can memorize and recite this sonnet, or one of Elizabeth Barrett Browning's poems, or I Corinthians 13 (the passage that everyone reads at weddings) over heart-shaped cupcakes after dinner on February 14.

St. Patrick's Day: *An Irish Blessing.* There are actually many Irish blessings (some of which are a little salty), but my favorite is:

> *May the road rise to meet you,*
> *May the wind be always at your back,*
> *May the sun shine warm upon your face,*
> *Rains fall soft upon your fields.*
> *And until we meet again*
> *May God hold you in the palm of His hand.*

Full disclosure: I am of Irish descent, and I have a little bit of an ax to grind regarding my desire for the rehabilitation of St. Patrick's reputation. He was an extraordinary man, born into wealth, then captured by pirates and sold to slave traders. When finally ransomed from slavery, he chose to return to his cruel oppressors to share with them the love and forgiveness of God. That's the kind of hero I want my kids to emulate, and he is a life worth celebrating. I don't really see the connection between this admirable character and drunks dressed like leprechauns wearing green face paint. But perhaps that will be addressed in another book.

Mark the holiday by doing something simple all together

Now that some of my kids are old enough to reminisce about their childhoods, it's interesting for me to hear what stands out in their minds regarding our family celebrations. Some of their favorite memories were very simple activities where we all joined in. For example:

On New Year's Day we make some popcorn and take out old family videos. It's a lot of laughs, and costs next-to-nothing.

On Thanksgiving before dinner we host a family two-on-two basketball tournament. Our son Steven always creates the brackets, pairing top-seeded players with those at the bottom to balance the teams. (Somehow I always get matched with our 6'4" son Davis, the family's best player!) Then, each team comes up with a name, costume and theme song. The competition is good-natured, and the winning team gets bragging rights for the year. (I once went down hard on a poorly-placed pick and had to serve dinner with a limp—but it was worth it!)

On Christmas Eve we hold a family talent show. Everyone has to perform (well, we give tiny babies a pass), and there have been some memorable acts: Grandpa singing in German, the toddler singing a never-ending version of "Jingle Bells," my son's girlfriend juggling, a teenager cranking out a gnarly version of "O Holy Night" on the electric guitar. You get the picture. It's the kindest audience you'll ever find.

On Christmas Day, after sunset, we all gather for a game: charades, Guesstures, or Signs. No skill required.

On the Fourth of July Eve (OK, I guess that's the Third of July) we walk to the park in the center of town and eat a picnic during the Holiday Concert. Although the music can be schmaltzy, and the whole event is pretty Mayberry, even the teenagers insist on attending.

On Easter afternoon we host a competitive egg hunt—not because eggs and John 20 have much to do with each other, but just because it's good family fun. We divide into two teams each with its own "territory." Unobserved by the opposition, each team hides two dozen eggs in its territory. After all the eggs are hidden, we invade the opposite team's turf to hunt out their eggs. The first team to find them all wins. Sometimes we find eggs in July.

On Sundays we all go to church together and sit in the same row. If you did not grow up going to a house of worship, you might want to think about it. Sooner or later your kids will start to ask you why we were put on earth. If they are grounded in a faith tradition, you have a starting point for the conversation. Attending weekly services together connects our family around something bigger than us. We also meet and learn to love all different kinds of people— folks from different countries, ethnic groups and income levels.

Simplicity is the key

It is easy let the burden of creating family traditions become an onerous weight that pulls you down. Don't let that happen. If there are traditions that you dread because they are so difficult to execute, cut them loose. Focus on simple foods and activities that are reserved for a special day and which draw the family together. Your traditions should have only enough weight to tether your kids' hearts to the family. That's a manageable weight.

Question #6:

WOULD YOU SHARE YOUR HOLIDAY RECIPES?

Why of course I would! There are millions of places to find great recipes, but for some reason, friends always ask for mine. My hunch is they want advice from the operator of a "test kitchen" who specializes in pleasing a broad range of ages and tastes. They also know that I don't spend all day in my kitchen, so my menus *must* be easy to execute.

Here are some of my holiday recipes, and I'll put some of my regular go-to meals on my website: stronghappyfamily.org. A few of the recipes are there right now, and I'll add more over time. When we have that cup of coffee together, I'll want to know yours!

HOLIDAY MENU RECIPES FOR FAMILY TRADITIONS

A St. Patrick's Day Feast

Corned beef, cabbage, potatoes, carrots, Irish soda bread and green milk

A corned beef, potatoes and cabbage dinner is about the easiest meal in the world to prepare. Pair it with my Mom's Irish Soda Bread recipe and you're practically in Dublin. If you think you don't like soda bread, try my Mom's recipe. I love it toasted with butter for breakfast. If you

want your kids to remember the meal forever, add several drops of green food coloring to the pitcher of milk and stir.

Corned Beef

There are two cuts of corned beef: point and flat. The point cut is more marbled, usually tastier, and often more expensive. The flat cut has less fat and flavor, but is probably a tad more healthful, and slices up better for sandwiches made from leftovers. I buy point, but flat cut makes a lovely dinner.

Open up a large corned beef along with the little seasoning packet that it's packaged with, and place them in a large pot half filled with water. Cover the pot and let it simmer on a low heat all day. (Really, at least six hours.) When it's done it should fall apart easily. Mmmmmm.

Boiled Potatoes, Carrots and Cabbage—All in one Pot!

Slice up some potatoes and carrots into bite-size pieces. (There's no need to peel them; the skins add to the meal's flavor.) Place them into a large pot of boiling water and cook on medium heat until the vegetables are tender. Then add a cabbage, cut into eight wedges and cook for another couple of minutes. Drain the contents of the pot into a colander, then replace the contents into the pot. Add a stick of melted butter (I always melt my sticks in a Pyrex measuring cup in the microwave first) and stir. Cover until you're ready to serve. (I serve right from the pot—the Irish way.)

Manny's Irish Soda Bread

- o   3 cups flour
- o   ½ cup sugar
- o   ½ teaspoon salt
- o   2 teaspoons caraway seeds
- o   ½ cup raisins
- o   1½ teaspoons baking soda
- o   1½ cups buttermilk

Combine all the dry ingredients, and then add the buttermilk. Mix and form the sticky dough into two balls. Place them on a cookie sheet, and bake at 350° for about an hour. (Your testing knife should come out dry.) When the loaves are done, drizzle them with honey.

Make sure you make enough loaves to have some for breakfast.

Now put on the Clancy Brothers or Switchback, and don't count calories today.

An April Fool's Day Dinner

Meatloaf cupcakes with mashed potato "frosting" and cookie pizza with fruit leather "toppings"

Nobody in our house gets fooled by this menu anymore, but it still makes us smile.

Meatloaf

- o   3 pounds of ground beef
- o   2 tablespoons salt
- o   1 tablespoon pepper
- o   10-ounce container of panko bread crumbs
- o   20-ounce jar of grape jelly
- o   6 eggs

Preheat the oven to 350°. Coat two muffin tins (24 muffins holes) with cooking spray. Mix all the ingredients. Form the meat into 24 balls and press them into the muffin tins. Bake for about 20 minutes. Remove the "cupcakes" from the oven, and let them cool slightly.

Mashed Potato Frosting

You can use instant potato flakes for this, or my trusty mashed potato recipe. You don't want soupy potatoes for this meal—they need to stand up of the job!

- o 5 pounds of potatoes (I like Yukon Gold) cut up
- o 1 stick of butter
- o 1 8-ounce package of cream cheese, room temp
- o ½ cup of milk (maybe a little more)
- o 1 teaspoon Knorr seasoning
- o Food coloring

Boil the potatoes until they are soft. Drain them into a colander, then return them to the pot. Combine milk, butter and Knorr seasoning in a large Pyrex measuring cup and microwave until the butter is melted. Add the mixture to the potato pot. Now add the softened cream cheese. (That will make the frosting stand up on your "cupcake," and make the taste buds stand up in your mouth!) Use a hand mixer to whip the potatoes.

If you'd like several different colors of potato "frosting," separate the potatoes into several small bowls and add a few drops of food coloring to each. If you're feeling adventurous, pipe the potatoes onto the meat muffins. Otherwise, just spread them on. Playfully arrange them on a cake stand or cupcake tree. Giggle with your kids.

Cookie Pizza with Gum Drop Toppings

We started making this before "cookie pizzas" were ubiquitous. It's still a lot of fun.

- o 1 package sugar cookie dough in a tube
- o 1 16-ounce can vanilla frosting
- o red, black, green, white, black and yellow gumdrops and fruit leather

65

Pat the cookie dough into a greased pizza pan. Bake until just golden brown. Let it cool.

Spread the cooled "pizza" with the frosting, leaving the "crust" unfrosted. Cut the gumdrops and fruit leather into shapes resembling pepperoni, green peppers, onions and mushrooms and top your pizza. Eat and laugh.

Fourth of July

Chicken Mango Salsa Flatbreads To Go

Every Independence Day our family walks to the center of our town, where the rest of the village also gathers, for a picnic concert. I've developed this very simple dinner for the event: it travels well, is easy to serve on a blanket, covers all the food groups, and is a snap to clean up in the dark. It's a picnic go-to recipe. I make homemade flatbreads for the special day (easy enough) but you can replace them with Naan—almost as good!

Chicken
- o 1 pound chicken tender strips
- o 2 tablespoons olive oil
- o 1 tablespoon spicy Montreal seasoning

Toss chicken in the olive oil and seasoning. Sauté or grill on a medium-low heat. Set aside. (If you're in a time crunch, you can substitute frozen breaded chicken strips. Just microwave them in the bag!)

Mango Salsa
- o   3 mangos, chopped
- o   5 chopped green onions (called scallions in some states)
- o   1 bunch of fresh cilantro, chopped
- o   juice of 1 lime
- o   1 tablespoon olive oil
- o   ½ teaspoon dried crushed chili peppers (optional)

Toss everything together. Set aside.

Grilled Flatbread

- o   2 cups warm water
- o   1 tablespoon sugar
- o   2 teaspoons active dry yeast
- o   8 tablespoons olive oil, plus more for brushing
- o   5-6 cups flour
- o   1 tablespoon sea salt, plus more for tossing

Mix warm water, sugar and yeast in a large bowl until the mixture bubbles. Add the rest of the ingredients, knead for a few minutes, then cover the bowl with a towel and let it sit for 2-3 hours.

Turn the griddle on to high, or crank up the barbecue grill. Grab a fist-sized ball of dough and flatten it out with your hands, or roll it with a rolling pin. (We like ours kind of thick, so I prefer to shape the loaf with my hands.) Brush both sides of the loaf with olive oil, then place it on the griddle, 2-3 minutes on the first side; 1-2 minutes on the second. Toss some sea salt on top of each loaf.

(If you use Naan instead of making your own flatbread, try warming the Naan right on your stove burner or the barbecue grill.)

Assembling the flatbreads:

Spread each flatbread with some whipped cream cheese (optional). Add two strips of chicken and a dollop of mango salsa. Fold the flatbread in half and wrap it in aluminum foil. Throw your flatbreads in a sack and go. Be sure to pack some for your neighbors.

Thanksgiving Day

Moist Thanksgiving Turkey, Best Gravy Ever and Mashed Potatoes Everyone Likes

Sooner or later, the lot falls on you, and you must make the Thanksgiving turkey. Many otherwise confident women panic at the thought of preparing "the bird," as they conjure childhood memories of sawdust-dry turkey meat. Cooking a moist turkey is not that hard. Let's just not let anyone in on our little secret:

- o   1 large turkey
- o   2 sticks of room temperature butter
- o   3 apples, cut in slices
- o   3 onions, cut in slices
- o   sage leaves (optional)
- o   salt and pepper to taste

1. Thaw your turkey out. Conscientious women thaw their turkeys for three days in the refrigerator. My mom always put hers out on the counter for 24 hours, and no one ever got sick—but you better stick with what it says on the label. Don't forget there are probably two packets of parts tucked into the cavity of the bird. Make sure you take those out.
2. With your hands, separate the turkey's skin from its breast meat. (Let your kids watch; it looks kind of creepy.) Spread both sticks of soft butter under the skin.
3. Stuff the apples, onions and sage inside the bird's cavity.
4. Place the bird in a large baking pan, and cover it with aluminum foil.
5. Cook at 350° for twenty minutes per pound. Remove the

aluminum for the last 30 minutes of cooking.

6. Place the bird on a channeled cutting board or rimmed cookie sheet, and let it stand for twenty minutes before carving. (Don't worry about carving it the "right" way. Nobody really cares.)
7. Keep all the buttery, fruity, oniony drippings to make the best gravy ever.

The Best Gravy Ever

When I first got married, my husband's grandmother and national treasure, Esther, offered to share with me her family's recipe for gravy:

> *"First pour about 4 ounces of white wine," she instructed.*

> *"Does this go in with the turkey drippings?" I asked.*

> *"No. Drink it. You'll need to fortify yourself for gravy-making."*

While Grammy's gravy was delicious, mine doesn't require any fortification. It's simple and very good. (I usually have a glass of wine anyway, in honor of Grammy!)

- o   ½ cup flour
- o   2 cups milk
- o   all the drippings from the turkey

1. Leaving the drippings in the baking pan, place the pan across two burners and turn the heat on low.
2. Mix the milk and flour together in a measuring cup and whisk with a fork.
3. Slowly add the flour and water mixture to the drippings and stir constantly.
4. If the gravy seems too thick, add more milk. If it seems too thin, make some more flour-milk mixture and add it. Salt and pepper to taste.

Your turkey will be moist enough that you won't need gravy, but you'll be glad you made it.

Mashed Potatoes Everyone Likes

I'm Irish. I love potatoes. And I love exotic variations on standard preparations: turnips and roasted garlic pureed in, or Gorgonzola crumbled throughout. But on Thanksgiving, I put my bag of tricks away, and make mashed potatoes everyone likes.

- o 10 pounds of Yukon Gold potatoes (you'll need to have some for leftovers tomorrow)
- o 1 pound of butter
- o 1-2 cups of whole milk (Skim will work, but it won't taste as good. Use half and half if you have the guts!)
- o 2 teaspoons sea salt
- o 1 teaspoon ground black pepper

1. I have never peeled my potatoes, so the kids have never been the wiser. I think the skins give the potatoes a satisfying chewiness. But if you can't pull it off, then go ahead and peel the potatoes. Then cut them into same-sized pieces.
2. Put the potatoes into a large pot of water and boil for 30-45 minutes.
3. Drain the potatoes in a colander, then return them to the pot.
4. Microwave the milk and butter until the butter melts, then pour the mixture over the potatoes.
5. Add salt and pepper to the potatoes.
6. Mix with a hand mixer or a masher. Adjust the seasoning.

You can put the potatoes in a buttered dish and refrigerate them for a few days if you want to make the potatoes ahead of time. Just bake the dish covered for about 30 minutes at 350° while the turkey is standing and being carved.

Christmas Lasagna

My people are Irish, but for some reason, my parents always served Italian food on the holidays. (Nobody ever complained about that!) On Christmas Day, after all the excitement of the morning activities, my mom would put out the enormous lasagna she had created a few days before, set out a big stack of plates and a pile of forks, and sit back for the afternoon and enjoy her family. Word of her lasagna got around, and eventually neighbors would come a-calling on Christmas afternoon and evening. Those were the best childhood memories, so I decided to take a leaf from my mother's book.

My lasagna construction is more simplified than my mother's, but the result is pretty satisfying. You can make it days in advance (in fact, it's tastier if you do), and it can tolerate sitting on a buffet table for hours. By three o'clock on Christmas Day, my feet are on the ottoman for keeps, and my kids (and many of their friends) are full and happy. Sadly, there are rarely Boxing Day leftovers.

Sauce:

- 8 large cans of crushed tomatoes
- ½ cup olive oil
- 2 tablespoons crushed basil
- 2 pounds of Italian sausage, out of the casings
- 2 tablespoons salt
- 2 tablespoons sugar

Instructions:

1. In a large pot, fry the sausage in the olive oil until it is cooked through.
2. Add the tomatoes, basil, salt and sugar.
3. Simmer for 3 or 4 hours, stirring occasionally.

Cheese Mixture:

- o   2 pounds of Ricotta cheese
- o   2 pounds of shredded mozzarella cheese
- o   8 eggs
- o   2 tablespoons of Italian seasoning

Mix well in a large bowl. Set aside. Now get out:

- o   2 boxes of lasagna noodles, uncooked (Don't buy the no-boil kind.)
- o   2 cups of water

Assembly:

1. Spray a large baking pan with non-stick cooking spray.
2. Ladle the sauce into the pan until the bottom is covered.
3. Line the bottom of the pan with uncooked lasagna noodles. (I can fit 5 noodles crosswise in my 12x18 pan.)
4. Spoon the cheese mixture onto each noodle, and spread with a spatula.
5. Repeat steps 2-4 until your ingredients run out. End with sauce.
6. Add two cups of water to the pan.
7. Cover with aluminum foil and bake at 350° for 1-2 hours, until the noodles are soft and the cheese is melty.
8. Let stand for 15 minutes before serving.

If you have the energy, toss a salad. Now enjoy your Strong Happy Family.

Question #7:

HOW DO YOU ORGANIZE YOUR HOME?

The great architect Louis Sullivan built a fabulous home in my neighborhood, so his dictum "Form ever follows function" always looms in my mind. Designing and organizing a peaceful home begins with a mental exercise that forces you to think through the function of each room. Before you dig in and do your overhaul, sit down and decide three things:

1. What will this room be used for?
2. How will I store or arrange the things that we use here?
3. How will the storage or arrangement be maintained?

Sullivan would admonish us to spend some time on question #1. At first glance, that seems like a question with obvious answers: we eat in the kitchen, we sleep in the bedroom, etc. But in reality, we do many different activities in each room of our homes. We might eat dinner, do homework, make crafts and pay the bills in the kitchen. Bedrooms might be for sleep, flute practice, TV watching and Legos. Thinking carefully about how you'd like each room in your home to function is the important first step in determining the form that your organizational systems will take.

In our home I lean toward narrowly defining the activities to be conducted in each room. For example, our living room is for reading, playing board games, or conversation. If you want to eat a sandwich, or check your Facebook, or paint your nails, there's a place for that— but it's not the living room. Since that room's functions are limited to those three activities, it tells me that there I need bookcases, a place to store board games, some good lighting, a large horizontal surface and comfy seating. (I do keep a hatbox full of lifelike toy animals on a living room shelf for my pre-reading, pre-gaming, pre-conversational guests. I want those little ones around!) Since we stick to those three activities in the living room, the place stays orderly and uncluttered, and people actually enjoy books, conversations and games there.

A brilliantly designed form-following-function room, however, only works if the organizational system is easy *for children* to maintain. Forget alphabetizing books and storing games on a high shelf. If kids don't understand your system, or can't physically operate within it, you are Sisyphus rolling the boulder up the hill. Don't design a room so that you are the only one who understands its logic, or the only one patient enough to maintain it. Even a visitor should be able to figure out how to pick up a room in your home.

Give kids a small storage space on each floor of your home

How it took me so long to figure this one out is beyond me! Every person in your household should have a place to stash his junk on *each floor* of your home. This increases the odds that a family member will indeed put his stuff away. And, on the off chance that a child should somehow forget to put a belonging away (you *are* reading all the intended sarcasm into that clause, aren't you?) you have a convenient place to toss it when you tidy.

We live in a 115-year-old house in the Chicago area, built at a time when the term "mud room" referred to the dirt floor cedar-shingled house down the street. In fact, our house originally didn't have a single closet on the first floor! To provide each kid with space on that level, I tucked a tall pantry-style kitchen cabinet in a hallway. It has twelve shelves, one for each of us, the taller you are, the higher your shelf. On the second floor, the kids each get one dresser to themselves for their clothing, and one drawer in their dresser is designated for their junk. (They would call their junk "treasures." I suppose it's in the eye of the beholder.) The third floor of our home doubles as our family room and schoolroom. There, the kids each have a drawer of a file cabinet to stash their school supplies and other personal effects.

Of course, all of those personal storage places do need to be sorted through regularly, but providing designated spaces for each family member reduces the number of panicky "three minutes 'til game time" baseball glove searches per season. It also keeps the stairs from piling high with items that can never quite make it to their homes on another floor. As a bonus, when kids have their own spaces, they feel more in-control of their lives, and take more responsibility for their possessions.

Organizing bedrooms

OK. I'm pretty much a failure on this one. My kids' bedrooms are eligible for FEMA funds. With a couple sets of bunk beds per room, and the complete wardrobe for each bedroom's inhabitants stored in said room, things can get messy. I console myself with the thought that it could be worse. In fact, it used to be worse, before I learned a few tricks.

First, bedrooms are for sleeping, dressing, and reading. (The parents' bedroom has one other permissible activity—wink wink.) No toys, repeat, no toys allowed! Add the jumble of toys to the jumble of clothes, and a child won't be able to play or dress. Also, no computers are allowed in kids' rooms—you are just asking for trouble there. (See the chapter in my upcoming book *Strong Happy Sons* on raising sane teenagers in sex-obsessed world.)

In my home, strewn clothing is the source of bedroom bedlam: clean clothes and dirty clothes, flagrantly cohabiting on the floor. To curtail it, I ask my kids to put their clean laundry away immediately upon carrying it up to their rooms. Then I provide an ample receptacle for their dirty clothes. Finally, I install clothes hooks wherever the stud finder will permit me. The large laundry bin and the ubiquitous hooks provide convenient destinations for removed clothing.

Sometimes it works.

Bathrooms— getting down to business

I love to page through interior design magazines. (It's all I do in the dentist's waiting room during the month each year I take my kids in for their dental appointments.) Those magazines feature spreads on bathrooms which look like they come from Versailles—if Louis XIV had had indoor plumbing. Knickknacks, accouterment and tchotchke abound. They're beautiful. And, for a large family, ridiculous.

Since in our home there is often a line to use the facilities, I don't want to encourage users to spend any more time there than necessary. Because our frequently-used bathrooms need to be cleaned daily, I don't want any extraneous surfaces to wipe. And since space is at a premium in a bathroom that must house a dozen towels and many rolls of TP, the joint needs to be clutter-free.

I stock our medicine cabinets and vanities with the basics: toothpaste, shaving cream, mouthwash, shampoo, etc. I have a few children who like to primp with specialty products, and I encourage those kids to bring a dop kit or toiletry bag to the bathroom with them— and take it away with them when they leave.

Towels are stacked high in our bathrooms. I have a strong bias toward white, lightweight cotton towels. They are inexpensive to buy (less than $2 each at Wal-Mart), easy to wash (you can bleach them 'til they smell clean), they air dry quickly (key to reducing mold in a frequently-used bathroom), and they match any decor (except maybe Versailles's). I hang rods and hooks wherever I can, and sweetly encourage my children to use them.

And speaking of sweet, no bathroom could be fully stocked without cleaning products. In our house, once a week the bathroom gets a thorough cleaning, where the toilet is scoured with bowl cleaner and the tub is scrubbed with Comet. I keep those harsh chemicals in a secure central location that only "big people" can access. But daily, the bathroom gets a once-over with Windex and paper towels. I still keep the Windex up high, but it is easily accessible to the designated daily bathroom custodian. (It's often the 12-year-old's job around here.) The daily wipe-down keeps the Health Department away.

Closets with no skeletons

As I mentioned before, my nineteenth century home doesn't have many closets, so I've had to make the most of what I have. For me, the key to efficiently utilizing the space lies in taking each closet apart annually. If you don't take your closets apart yearly, you might think that this would be an arduous ritual. Actually, the yearly check-up makes it a quick twenty-minute job.

Start by defining what exactly each closet will be used for. Think carefully about how that closet will serve you best. If it's by your front door, then it's for coats and outerwear, and perhaps the board games need to be evicted. If it's near the bathroom, then linens and toiletries hold the lease, and those hand-me-downs need to find lodging elsewhere.

Next, take everything out! The first time you do this, it will be a mess, but it will be worth it. Ruthlessly toss or relocate items that are not frequently used. If I am unsure about whether to dispose of something, I put it in a "holding pen" in an obscure, inaccessible corner of the basement. If I find during the subsequent year that I retrieve it, it re-earns a more accessible address. If it lingers unmolested for a year, off to Goodwill it goes!

Inside the closet, group like items according to their use. Matching baskets or bins give the closet a clean, organized look, and actually inspire users to keep the place organized. On the shelves of the closet that we added near the kitchen of our house, I keep big white plastic bins, clearly labeled for the following: "First Aid," "Batteries, extensions, flashlights, light bulbs," "Tools and tape," "Cleaning supplies," "Poisons," "Haircut equipment," and "Shoe care." Your priority list of bins might be different from mine, but nothing beats having logical categories of things you use often in an easily accessible location. And sorting through a bin each year is a piece of cake.

If your home is closet-deprived like mine, you might invest in some closet substitutes. An old wardrobe I found for $10 at a garage sale holds all our sleeping bags and guest pillows. I keep all our art supplies in an IKEA architect's cabinet featuring 20 drawers. Steel shelving lines the walls of my basement, and holds bins of lower-priority or off-season items. Handsome oak dressers (yes, acquired at garage sales—I'm a bit of a junkie) make terrific living room accent pieces, and can house board games, blankets and candles.

Wherever your storage spaces are found, make the most of them by keeping them uncluttered, organized and labeled.

Designing, then organizing a kitchen

When my tenth child was born, I was doing all my cooking in a butler's galley kitchen that featured a two-burner stove. When we finally decided to transform our old family room into a large kitchen, I was eager to talk with experts about how to design the space. I soon realized, however, that most kitchen design experts knew either how to make a kitchen beautiful, or how to make it functional for a family of four. I wanted a beautiful kitchen that worked for twelve or more people, three meals a day, seven days a week. I stumped them.

Through lots of thinking and experimenting, I came up with a design that has really worked, and still looks good. What's more, I think the principles employed would make a great kitchen for a family of four.

My kitchen design strategy centered on a large, counter-height island with an overhang, around which the whole family could sit on stools for most of its meals. Stools are the best because when they're not being sat upon, they tuck under the countertop to provide unobstructed workspace. The island hosts a sink with a dishwasher alongside, and when a meal is complete, the eaters simply push their plates and utensils toward the sink for a quick and easy cleanup. When the dishwasher cleaning cycle is complete, the next meal's table can be set directly from the dishwasher. On the other side of the sink are large *drawers* to hold plates, bowls and utensils. Having everything necessary to set and clean up a table within easy reach for kids makes it simple to delegate those jobs to them.

My kitchen designers recommended that I buy one of those enormous Sub-Zero refrigerators. I saw a few problems with that: First, for many families, they can be ridiculously expensive to buy and repair. Second, an enormous refrigerator has an enormous door, which occludes passageways in a kitchen. The last thing I want to do in my kitchen is keep people from helping me. And of course, keeping all my perishables in a central location could cause logjams if helpers are working on several jobs at once.

I opted for buying two reasonably-priced, regular-sized refrigerators. The doors are narrow, so you can pass by when one is open, and I can split categories of food between them. I keep all lunchmeats and sandwich fixings in the fridge right by the bread drawer, and all salad components in the fridge near the cutting boards, knives and salad bowls. Since the kids are always looking for a cold drink just about the time I am fixing dinner, I keep refreshments in a separate fridge from the fridge that holds ingredients I often use to make supper. That keeps the cook happy.

If you are able to squeeze a second sink (and second dishwasher) into your design, I endorse that idea! Two sinks and dishwashers double the speed of a meal cleanup, since people can be deployed at two workstations. It also permits two separate menu projects to be conducted simultaneously. If a second dishwasher seems extravagant to you, remember this: a dishwasher costs less than a kitchen cabinet. You could always store your dishes there!

I am very glad that I chose a large, no-frills range for the kitchen. I don't need lots of bells and whistles, but I do need to be able to cook six frozen pizzas at once. I have been so grateful to be able to bake a dozen dozen cookies in an hour or to prepare all the pork butts for the graduation party's pulled pork in one session. (Look for the pulled pork recipe on my website. No child should graduate without it.)

Designer kitchens have beautiful cabinets to hold garbage receptacles. Hmm. That means two hands are required to throw anything away. I don't think so. I want a huge tough plastic garbage bin that can travel with me around the kitchen. Dinner prep? Move it to the cooking station. Dinner clean up? Move it to the table. Save the cabinet space for more important things.

And speaking of cabinet space, don't forget to look up. Storing items in high cabinets or atop wall cabinets might require a stool to access, but it is great space. Since I don't go to a gym, I consider dinner prep to be my Stairmaster class. Keeping most of your ingredients and equipment in one room helps with the creative flow, so it's worth the climb. (Look for more about simultaneously keeping your house and your figure in shape in a future title!)

Toy madness

When you have little children, a huge factor in creating a peaceful home is managing toys. Toy clutter can drive even the most mild-mannered mother wild. And when toys are strewn and unorganized, kids don't enjoy them. If you don't create a system to manage toys, both you and your children can be miserable.

In preparation for remodeling our attic family room/playroom/schoolroom some years ago, I had to pack up almost all of the toys into boxes. After the boxes were sealed and stacked, we hit a financial setback. A protracted financial setback. In fact, it was several years before we were able to complete the project.

Guess how many times my kids asked for their toys during those years? Zero. When their beloved playthings were out of sight, they were out of mind. The kids moved on to sports and art projects and baking and inventing their own toys.

When it was finally time to unpack those boxes, I had some new ideas about organizing the toy room! First, the toys didn't get their own room. They got a walk-in closet under the eaves with a slanting ceiling, high enough for little ones, but otherwise unusable for adults.

Next, I instituted the "Five Toy Rule." I identified five toys that had withstood the test of time, that engaged kids' minds for prolonged periods of time, and that could be easily expanded. Since my five youngest children are all boys, my five toys were: Lego, Duplos,

Playmobil, Capsella and Darda cars. (If I had had girls in the mix, I think I would have substituted kitchen equipment for Capsella, and baby doll supplies for Darda.)

Finally, I got five huge storage bins with lids and labeled them with the names of the five toys. Those bins lined up neatly against the wall, and their lids became a work surface for the kids' creations.

My new system revolutionized cleanup time! No five-year-old in the world can look at a jumbled pile of plastic and sort it into two dozen categories. But even a three-year-old can sort the pile into five groups. Since I created a system that my little children could manage, the toy room stays organized and welcoming. The kids actually want to go there and get lost in their imaginary worlds. Without the chaos of clutter, the toy room is their creative refuge—which buys me some peace when it's time to make dinner!

When Christmas or birthdays come along, we give our kids gifts in those five categories. A new Lego spaceship or some extra Darda track rejuvenates the whole bin, and rekindles the kids' enthusiasm for what they already own. And of course, it fits right into the bin!

There are always miscellaneous toy items: Kids sometimes receive from friends or relatives gifts that don't follow the Five Toy Rule. I have always kept a little basket of baby toys on each floor of the house. And I am a bit of a sucker for Play Doh. (Play Doh, by the way, is an outdoors or kitchen toy at my house.) But your system can flex with a few extraneous items. The key is to create a system that the kids maintain by themselves.

Keeping your sanity: less is more

I suppose a running theme of my home organization is "Less is more." That is easier said than done. In a large family, it only makes sense to save clothing to pass on to younger kids. Many kids means many interests, each of which carries its own paraphernalia. To wit: I own soccer cleats, baseball cleats, and ice skates in every size, Youth 12 to Adult 12. There is a certain amount of inventory that needs management, but to the extent that you can pare down, do it!

Question #8:

WHAT DO YOU DO ABOUT LAUNDRY?

If there is one chore that hangs over moms, taunting them with its ubiquity and depressing them with its drudgery, it is the laundry. No matter what you do, it just keeps coming. The piles lie in corners, mocking you with their odors and reminding you of the time that they will steal from you. You want to give up, but you can't, because naked kids are just not a viable option.

Though I cannot say that I love doing the laundry, I have found a few ideas that have helped me tame the beast. After decades of washing muddy football uniforms, soiled crib sheets, teenage girls' costume changes, dirt-encrusted sleeping bags and other wash day delights, I've learned a trick or two. I offer them here in the hopes that they may lighten your load as you manage your loads.

Clothing choices

I love clothes (and shoes too.) I revel in creating iterations of myself by varying my wardrobe—one day classic Ann Taylor, the next day funky Urban Outfitters. But one thing most of my wardrobe has in common is the "NO IRON" icon. That goes double for kids' clothes.

Life is too short to iron.

Choosing your family's clothing to be low-care is the first step in reducing your laundry sentence. Wrinkle-free is a good start. Also choosing items that don't show stains easily, like denim and dark colors, can save you pre-treating time. I try to buy only one brand and style of sport socks to reduce sorting time. And I'm a big advocate of the simple cheap white towel, twenty of which can fit into one load.

Dresser limitations

In our house, each child gets one dresser, plus a little shared space in a closet. That means everyone needs to exercise restraint when it comes to wardrobe size. The unintended (and deviously beneficial) consequence of this space rationing is that the size of any one person's laundry load is restricted. You just can't wash what you don't own! Because of this, kids tend to wear the same pair of jeans a few times, and they don't just toss a sweatshirt in the hamper because that's easier than hanging it up. They put it away, because they know they'll need it tomorrow.

Little children tend to have a few favorite outfits they like to wear anyway. Instead of stuffing their drawers with clothes they don't prefer, just work with them. Let them wear those few little outfits, and accept the empty space in the laundry basket as a gift.

Workspace

In magazines, I've seen photos of amazing laundry rooms. Some are as big as a family room and feature large folding tables, beautiful clothing racks, supply cabinets, ironing stations, and enormous lockers dedicated to each family member. With ten kids, we don't wish to spare a whole room just for laundry. (In our house, if there's an extra room, someone throws a mattress in it and calls dibs on the space as a bedroom.) My "laundry room" is just a washer, a dryer, and a utility sink tucked into a corner of my kitchen behind a set of folding doors. I really like having the laundry room in a convenient place so I can chip away at the dirty clothes between other household chores.

I prefer a side-by-side washer/dryer arrangement, as opposed to stacked units. The side-by-side appliance tops make a perfect table for folding clothes. Over the appliances are two sets of shelves that hold baskets, a rarely-used iron and laundry supplies: detergent, bleach, stain treatment, and dryer sheets. Tucked next to the dryer is a small ironing board that can sit atop a table. Under the utility sink is a hamper. The space has as many hooks as it can hold. When one of my kids brings me a basket of dirty laundry, I can process it start-to-finish without taking a step. The space is compact, organized— and it really works!

If your laundry room is in a dismal place, try your best to brighten it up. You'll spend many hours of your life there, so make the most of it. If you're in the basement, try painting the floor white or some bright playful color. Cover the walls with beautiful prints or photos of the kids. If it's dark, maybe you could increase the wattage in your light fixtures, and even add a floor lamp. And why not plug in a radio or iPod dock? Some great music or an engaging lecture (my favorites are "The Great Courses" from The Teaching Company) can engage your intellect, giving you a little "vacation of the mind" with every load.

Choose a day

My attack strategy for the dirty duds is to choose one day a week to be my intensive laundry day. I start early in the morning, and attend to it regularly throughout the day. I make no appointments, and don't even allow the kids to have friends over that day. Finishing all the wash in one day is a challenge, but getting it over and done with is so gratifying!

My mom always did laundry on Mondays, and for some reason I just copied her. It turns out, she was brilliant. Sunday is a day of rest around here, so on Monday morning, my batteries are charged and ready for the challenge. You can choose any day that works for you, but having one day regularly dedicated to the task allows you to work the rest of your week's schedule around it.

There will, of course, be mid-week laundry emergencies: bed sheet accidents, three-day tournaments, and dishtowel shortages might force you to do an extra load here or there. But tackling the bulk of the laundry on a designated day allows you to rest on your laurels for the balance of the week.

Baskets, baskets, baskets

The bottoms of our bedroom closets are lined with cheap, white plastic baskets. Dirty clothes get tossed into the waiting baskets all week long. On Mondays, the baskets are brought down to the laundry room, the contents are processed, and then returned right into those same baskets. When the clean clothing is placed into drawers, the baskets are returned to the bottom of the closet. Sweet and simple.

Kids do the hauling

If you have healthy kids who are five or older, do not—I repeat—do not haul laundry for them! That is one chore they can certainly handle on their own. If a child is too little to carry a basket on his own, I assign an older kid to help.

I try to work on one bedroom's laundry at a time to minimize the post-folding sorting job. As soon as that room's laundry is complete, I have the kids haul it away. (Who needs to keep looking at that?) The oldest child in the room sorts the basket into piles for each of that room's inhabitants, and they are instructed to put their piles away *immediately*. Easier said than done, but the faster they put their piles away, the less likely it will be for those piles to wind up in a clothing collage on the floor.

I also have a go-to child for hauling towels and other non-personal effects. There is enough skilled labor involved with clothing care that mom doesn't need to be a part of the carting crew.

Kids who don't do their part

Perhaps like me, you have a non-compliant child in the laundry department. I find my boys in particular don't care much about rumpled clothing and not being able to find a shirt to match their shorts. They are happy to let their clean laundry consort on the floor with their rank raiment. I could insist that they keep a perfectly tidy room (and some of my sons do), but when they reach the teen years, I choose not to fight that battle. If they don't care about their clothing, then neither shall I.

If one of my teenagers will not put his laundry away promptly, then he is on his own. His laundry service is discontinued. I permit him to use the laundry room, so long as he's in and out quickly, and *never* on a Monday. At age eighteen, their laundry service is cut off completely.

Just do it

At the risk of sounding like a sneaker ad, you must summon the fortitude to just do the laundry. Nothing is gained by post-poning it. As Homer told Marge, "Don't worry. All your work will be waiting for you when you get back." Work it into the baseline, make it a non-negotiable, get it done, and reward yourself by not entering the laundry room again for six days! You'll be happy for your Strong Happy Family.

Question #9:

HOW DO YOU GET THROUGH A MISCARRIAGE?

(Many women dealing with despair after an abortion may appreciate this chapter too. If you are struggling after a chemical or surgical abortion, there is a special note for you at the end of the chapter.)

Miscarriages are devastating. Your own body becomes the tomb for a person whom you long to hold, but can't. Sometimes all there is to show for the life you had cherished in your heart is agonizing pain and rivers of blood. Sometimes you even see a little body. Your hormones, which had been ramped up to knit together a little person suddenly crash, leaving you feeling empty and dead inside.

Then a week later, well-meaning friends will ask you if you're over it. Over it? Over it? You want to scream at them. My child is gone. I will never hold her. I never got to say goodbye. My body is mourning in blood.

Then the platitudes begin: "Well, you'll have other children." (I'm not sad about others; I'm sad about *this* baby.) "At least it's not your first." (How in the world does birth order lessen my pain?) "Maybe it's for the best; your kids would have been too close in age." (Am I supposed to be comforted by that?) "You were kind of young (or old) to have a baby." (I'm dying, and you think that will help?)

Then after a month, you are expected to forget that you were ever pregnant. You are supposed to pretend that your baby never existed. Talk about it, and you're considered obsessed.

Your loss is real

If you have lost a child at any point in pregnancy or childhood, you have experienced an excruciating trauma. Don't let anyone dismiss your grief or minimize your loss. The bond between a mother and child is eternal, and a rending of that relationship leaves a gaping wound in your soul. Trying to convince yourself that there's no wound won't lead to healing. Ignoring a lacerated artery doesn't promote healing, and neither will dismissing a wounded soul.

First and foremost, you must acknowledge that there has been a death. You can't begin to grieve for your little one if you deny that she lived. Some women find it helpful to name their lost baby. If you didn't know your baby's gender, that might not seem right to you. But recognizing that what you're experiencing is grief over a death, and not just hormonal ragings, validates your process.

And then you must remember that grief *is* a process. If you lost your mother, no one would expect you to be "over it" in a month. The grieving process, though it lessens in intensity over time, can take years. After my first miscarriage I cried every day for a year. At first I cried all day long. Later it became less frequent, but it was still a daily event. Now, years later, I will still shed a tear from time to time over that little one.

Give yourself permission to weep. My dear friend Gwen, who had lost a baby to miscarriage herself, sent me a note after my first loss. Her words "Let the tears come," touched my soul and gave me the permission to do what I needed to do—grieve my loss. If you have a hard time giving yourself permission, I now grant it to you: *Cry your heart out.* Each tear that falls starts to mend that gushing wound in your soul.

Resist the temptation to deaden the pain with meds or other substances. Every time you avoid grief by taking something, you push back the end of the process. Your child has died. You should be sad. If you are not, there is something wrong with you. Don't let people tell you that you are sick. You are grieving.

Warning: there are two bad days coming

If you're like most of us, your grief year will contain two really bad days. Knowing in advance that they will be tough will help you know that you're not going crazy. It will also keep you from worrying that your grief is moving in the wrong direction.

One of your bad days will be the baby's due date. Your body's internal clock and your brain's external clock will both keep track of this day. I know this sounds crazy, but I have gone into mild labor on a lost baby's due date. It's almost as if your body, which nurtured that baby for a time, wants to create a memorial event for the child. You might want to schedule your day lightly on the due date.

The other tough day will be Mother's Day. This is particularly hard because there are so many joyful people on Mother's Day. If your mom is alive, or if you have other children, you'll feel an obligation to be "up" for them. I give you permission to take that Mother's Day off. Next year's won't feel so bad, and you can make up for it then.

Hope beyond grief

Your grief will run its course. The tears will become fewer and fewer, and the bad days will space themselves out. But just knowing that you will feel less sad in the future is sort of an empty comfort. If you are a mother who has lost a child, you long for reunion. No comfort is truly adequate unless it offers the hope of seeing that child face to face, and holding her in your arms.

I believe that we have that hope.

The Bible is a revered book in many of the world's major religions, and its message of hope is considered authoritative by millions. It says what we all know in our souls: that this is not the end. We have a sense that who we are, the essence of our being, is not limited to the cells that make up our bodies. We know that our souls will persist. But the Bible makes an even more audacious claim: It says that our bodies will be brought back to life.

If you are not deeply grieving the loss of a loved one, that claim may seem academic. If, however, you are in the throes of heartbreak, that promise is life to your spirit. The hope that you will one day see that little one, cradle her in your arms and have that longing in your heart finally fulfilled is soothing balm to a tortured soul. It reassures you that, just like the labor of delivery leads to life, the labor of grief will bear fruit as well.

It is very tempting, living in a country where I have all my earthly needs met, not to think very much about the non-material world. I can easily fill my days with planning meals and shuttling kids to practices, and even volunteering my time. But when a piece of my heart is torn out and placed somewhere else, I become intently focused on that somewhere else. Having a little one "on the other side," as my Irish relatives would say, makes me look forward to what lies beyond. Within a hundred years, you and I will both be gone, and what's on the other side will be our reality. As sad as I was to lose children before they were born, knowing that they are alive and that I will be united with them makes me less occupied with meaningless busyness. My vision now has a longer focus, and I care more about things that will really last.

If you want to read for yourself about life on the other side, here are some places in the Bible to start:

- Job 19:25-27
- Isaiah 53
- Daniel 12
- John 11
- Romans 6-8
- I Corinthians 15

One of my favorite parts of the Bible is, "We do not grieve like those who have no hope (I Thessalonians 4:13)." My grief is a real, painful process mourning the loss of someone eternally valuable. But it is a grief *with* hope—the hope of a mother and child reunion. As you and I are sisters in grief, I hope we can now also be sisters in hope.

A Note for Women Struggling After an Abortion

If you are experiencing despair or sadness after an abortion, all of the words in this chapter are for you. You need to grieve the baby who is gone, and set your hope on the reunion that is to come.

If you have experienced an abortion, you might also be dealing with guilt. Your soul is now telling you that the bond you had with your baby is eternal, and that it was wrong to have severed it.

The very good news is that the same God who will one day reunite you to your baby is standing ready to forgive you, and unite you to Himself. Just as you must acknowledge your baby's life in order to grieve her, you have to acknowledge your error in order to be forgiven. Romans 1:9 says, "If we confess our sins, He is faithful and just to forgive us our sins, and to cleanse us from all unrighteousness." Further, Psalm 103:12 says, "As far as the east is from the west, so far has he removed our transgressions from us." Go to God, admit your wrongdoing, and experience the joy and relief that comes from being forgiven. "The Lord is gracious and compassionate, slow to anger and rich in love (Psalm 145:8)."

He has promised that He will forgive those who call on Him. Don't call Him a liar.

Question #10:

HOW DO YOU GIVE YOUR KIDS A SENSE OF MEANING AND PURPOSE?

Your child is a spiritual being. All human beings are. Throughout history, in every culture, people have recognized that they are part of something bigger than themselves. Man's quest for spirituality is his search for how he fits into the big picture. Our innate yearning for significance stems from our inborn sense that our lives *do* matter in the cosmos, and we long to figure out our place.

Your child may not vocalize those ideas, but he knows that he was created. Since children are closer to the point of their own creation than we are, the idea seems quite natural to them. They also sense that they are beholden to their Creator; since they are dependent on their parents for everything, the idea of depending on God comes naturally to them too.

As a child grows, he will want to know about his Creator—who He is and what He expects. If his parents don't begin answering his questions for him, he will look to others for the answers. This is very scary, because there are many evil or deluded people who are eager to share their "answers."

I have a friend we'll call Caroline who had religious beliefs of her own, but she was very reluctant to share her faith with her daughter Annaliese. Caroline felt that if she talked too much about what she believed, Annaliese would feel pressured into "accepting" a faith she had not genuinely embraced. She wanted to respect her daughter's right to make up her own mind. She felt the enlightened approach would be to say nothing about religion and let her daughter start with a blank slate to figure things out on her own. And so my friend kept her faith to herself, and Annaliese's questions went unanswered. For a while.

Since Annaliese is a spiritual being, and since her spirit longed to know why she mattered in the universe, she took her questions to friends. They told her that that haunting conviction at the root of her being was wrong: She was not created. There is no God. She is an accident of time, matter and chance. Her life is meaningless.

Annaliese's initial reaction was to doubt her friends. Her soul kept telling her that she mattered, and that she was part of something very big and important. But she had no intellectual ammunition to combat what her friends were telling her. Her mom hadn't offered her a hopeful worldview, so she didn't have a reply. All she had was her gut, and she was smart enough to know you can't build your life around a feeling.

Annaliese adopted the nihilism of her friends, and that empty, hopeless worldview led her to some "rational" choices. She began to abuse drugs and drink a lot: A hopeless universe hurts, and she needed something to numb the pain. She dropped out of school: If what I do won't matter in a century, or even tomorrow, then why bother working hard to try to achieve something? She began to be promiscuous: If life didn't mean anything, then sex couldn't have a spiritual component. An accidental, pointless universe would be a dark, lonely place; maybe lots of random sex could ease the ache?

When Caroline finally figured out what was happening to her precious daughter, she wanted to die. She had withheld from Annaliese, out of respect for her daughter's "right to choose her own faith," the very information that would have freed her from the agony of living in a hopeless world.

Annaliese hadn't needed intellectual deference. She had needed a hopeful worldview by which to orient her life, a compass pointing her in the right, purposeful direction. She needed to know why she sensed in her soul that there was a God, and she had the right to know who He was. Caroline might not have shared her faith perfectly with her child, but she could have given her a starting point from which to learn. Pascal said that within each of us is a God-shaped void, and we all spend our lives trying to fill it. Annaliese's void-filling nearly killed her. God would have fit much better.

What faith?

I am a Christian, so the only first-hand experience I have in sharing my faith with my children is within the Christian tradition. I will share with you what I have done, hoping that the principles and techniques I describe might have application for you as you share your faith with your child.

If you really don't have a faith to speak of, why not explore with your children? The Bible is a great starting place, since it is a sacred book in so many of the world's religions. You don't need to commit upfront to a particular tradition; just start to see what the Bible has to say about our meaning and significance. I guarantee it, you will enjoy the journey with your children. It will also prepare your kids for lit classes in college! Most of the cherished novels of the Western canon are rife with biblical allusions. If you want your kids to understand the Great Books of Western Civilization, they need to have some biblical literacy!

How do I start?

I don't recommend jobbing this one out. This topic is way too important to trust to some volunteer (or professional) at the local house of worship. There might be some resources there for you to tap, but the nuts and bolts of this is going to have to be the parents' job. As wise men from Moses to Crosby, Stills and Nash advise: "Teach your children well."

The important first step is to carve out time in your schedule. See if you can find a fifteen-minute slot to claim daily when you can gather your children to share and learn about your faith. For many years my preferred time was at the breakfast table when I had a "captive audience." (The toddler in the high chair was literally a captive, and that would be the only time of the day when he would sit for fifteen minutes!) If you start to do this when your kids are young, they will just assume all families do this. Even if you begin when they are older, they will adjust and actually look forward to this time of the day.

The content of our Bible time together has been rich and varied through the years. Depending on our time constraints, and the ages of our kids, our times together have included:

Songs

Children love to sing, and they can memorize songs almost effortlessly. I like to choose a variety of songs, some that are peppy and playful, others that are contemplative and sacred. I make sure that the kids learn all of the verses of patriotic songs, some of which are very reverent hymns. Sometimes, I'll make a list of things I want the kids to memorize, and put it to music to help them learn the list quickly. (At stronghappyfamily.org I will list some Bible Literacy Songs.) As the kids got older, we tried to incorporate a musical instrument or learn a basic harmony. Now, with hundreds of song verses committed to memory, the kids have a little rhyming theology primer stored in their heads.

Memorizing

Modern folk have largely eschewed the time-honored practice of memorizing great literature. In times past, a Jewish boy would memorize the first five books of the Torah (Genesis, Exodus, Leviticus, Numbers and Deuteronomy) before his Bar Mitzvah. *The Iliad* and *The Odyssey* were each performed from memory by nomadic bards. When we don't teach our children to memorize beautiful, lyrical literature, we deny them an effective developmental tool. When children memorize, not only do they learn vocabulary and syntax, they also develop a forceful command of the language. The studied author's words weave into the warp and woof of their own minds, germinating big ideas.

In our times together, my kids and I have memorized from Psalms and Proverbs, Jesus' venerated Sermon on the Mount, speeches by Abraham Lincoln, George Washington and Thomas Paine, poems by Longfellow, Shelley and Shakespeare, and important Bible passages like the Ten Commandments and the Lord's Prayer. Often, in the middle of the day, one of my children will ask me about a passage that we had been trying to commit to memory earlier that morning. I can tell that the lovely words have been swirling in my child's head, beckoning him to think big thoughts and own powerful ideas.

Bible Reading

If you've never read the Bible before, you'll be pleasantly surprised to find out what an interesting book it is. It is full of adventure, espionage, mystery, sex, envy, betrayal, more sex, heroism, violence, redemption and sex. Many people pick up a Bible with the noble intention of reading it through. Then, ten chapters in, they hit a genealogy, give up for lost, and never venture to return. (Genealogies in the Bible are a lot like phone books; they serve a useful purpose, but they're not very interesting reading.)

If you and your kids are novices at Bible reading, start with narrative books such as I Samuel, II Samuel, Esther, Ruth, Mark, Luke or Acts. Books like John and Psalms have a beautiful, lyrical quality, and rest easily on the ears.

Recently, I downloaded on my iPhone the free app Bible.is. With it you can hear the whole Bible, in over 100 different languages (with five different English translations) all read by trained actors with engaging music and sound effects in the background. My kids love it (and I do too).

Often when we read the Bible together, my kids will ask me to explain what we just read. Sometimes I think I know the answer; other times I'm stumped and I have to research an answer for them later. But the very process of looking into big ideas together creates a bond in your family. Don't be discouraged if you feel like you don't understand very much of the Bible. You'll be surprised how, bit-by-bit, it will begin to make sense to you. And I think you'll find, for your children and yourself, that you start to have answers to some of life's big questions.

After you've read the more narrative books of the Bible, you might be curious to read some of the prophets or the more doctrinal books. These are wonderful works, but sometimes a bit challenging for children or the unacquainted. To tackle those books initially, I recommend using one of two superb volumes that synthesize the contents of those books, and connect all the necessary cross-reference material for you. The first is Catherine F. Vos's *The Child's Story Bible*, a sweetly narrated retelling of the whole Bible penned in 1935. The other is *Hurlbut's Story of the Bible*. See if you can pick up an original version of Jesse Lyman Hurlbut's 1904 classic; it's full of gorgeous plates. (For your convenience, you can order these and other books I've found helpful from my website stronghappyfamily.org under the "Resources" tab.) Both of these titles were written back in the day before children's authors thought kids were idiots. They use an engaging, respectful voice and draw children in with rich, accurate content. If you read a story a day aloud to your children, you could easily finish either of these books in a school year. By the end of that year, you'll really start to understand the major themes and the narrative flow of the whole Bible. (Then you'll start to understand 19th century poetry!)

Prayer

Prayer is something that seems very foreign to many people. It is often "left to the professionals." But if you want your kids to understand that they were created by, and are beholden to, Someone much greater than themselves, who loves them deeply—and if that Someone has actually asked you to communicate with Him, then why not?

For many people, it is helpful at first to pray formal, written prayers. "The Shema," "The Our Father," "The Act of Contrition," or a standard prayer of thanksgiving are all meaningful and full of devotion. Many of the chapters of the Book of Psalms in the Bible are just prayers, originally put to music. As you and your children become more comfortable with the idea of speaking to God, you can encourage your children to voice their own concerns or gratitude. I often pray aloud with my children, reminding them to acknowledge God for who He is, to confess their shortcomings, to thank Him for His gifts, and to ask Him for what is on their hearts.

Attending a house of worship

In most faith traditions, believers are encouraged to gather together. When I meet with other believers at church, my faith is strengthened, and my children are reminded that they are not the only ones who believe in God. Seeing peers who also acknowledge their Creator bolsters their faith. The congregation is a place where my husband, kids and I have met people we might never have run into otherwise: homeless folks, Ph.D. candidates from China, Coptic refugees from Egypt, Nigerian families who left everything to come to America, Romanians released from Ceausescu's gulag, ex-cons from downstate, recovering drug addicts and alcoholics, kids with Down's syndrome and teenage mothers. We also meet people who are doing amazing, inspiring things: tutoring inner-city kids, working to stop human trafficking, feeding the hungry, clothing the poor, adopting abandoned kids, opening hospitals in Central America, building wells in Africa, caring for elderly parents, advocating for the voiceless. Being around people like that makes our faith bigger, and challenges us to do great things. When kids lie in bed at night and wonder what their part in the great story of the universe is, they might look to wonderful role models they meet at their house of worship to get some ideas.

Live it like you mean it

The most effective way to share your faith with your kids is to live it. In America we have strangely morphed the genius of our First Amendment that guarantees freedom of religion, to somehow conclude that we must isolate our religion so that it won't influence our lives. This is crazy. A vibrant, healthy faith will inform all aspects of your life, from your appreciation of the arts, to the decisions you make at work. A faith that is segregated to Sunday mornings or Friday evenings is not too useful for answering life's big questions. If you practice a one-hour-a-week faith, your kids will think you are a hypocrite. Kids despise hypocrites.

Kids long to see demonstrated a faith that permeates their parents' lives, shedding light on their decisions and giving them hope in crises. Kids want to know that their parents have anchored their souls in a robust faith that is able to withstand intellectual scrutiny. And they want to see that their parents have the courage to live out their convictions day to day.

If you want to share your faith with your kids, live it out. Let your faith be evident in how you choose your entertainment, and how you treat your employees, and how you spend your money. Don't let them see a disconnect between what you say you believe, and how you treat the clerk at the grocery store. If kids perceive you own a faith that is powerful enough to infiltrate every area of your life, it will make them curious.

AFTERWORD

I hope this little glimpse into our Strong Happy Family encourages you, or at least gives you a couple of ideas to tuck into your back pocket (next to the spare diaper and zip-lock full of Cheerios). As I mentioned in the Introduction, not all of the ideas are for every family. If you're a single parent, or have a disabled child, or a difficult marriage, or a deployed spouse, or any other tough challenges, some of the ideas in this book might not be useful to you. Please don't think I'm trying to set a standard for you to live up to: I've only wanted to try to answer the questions I'm asked—and to share some ideas that have lightened my load, in the hope that those ideas might do the same for you.

There are lots of questions I haven't answered, ones like "How do you keep your marriage alive during the baby years?" or "How do you go about potty training?" or "How do you keep kids' activities in balance?" or "What do you do with rebellious kids?" or "How do you care for aging parents when you're still caring for young kids?" or "How do you help kids choose (and pay for!) college?" or "How do you do vacations?" or "How do you keep the kids from fighting with each other?" or "How do you teach them about sex?" or "How do you get by on just one income?" Look for those topics in an upcoming title!

When I was a young mother, I used to get annoyed when older moms would say, "Cherish these fleeting years with your kids—they will be over so soon." That admonition seemed so whimsical; was I supposed to sit placidly in the chaos and squalor, smiling wanly at the toddler's tantrum while snuggling in a mountain of dirty laundry? The advice to "cherish" didn't give me the encouragement—or the game plan— I needed to get me through my nearly insurmountable daily tasks. The years might indeed fly by, but the afternoons last *forever—figuratively.*

So here is my advice to you: Go all in. Leave nothing on the table. Be a parent at full throttle.

You will get tired— but you will get tired no matter how you choose to spend your time. (Even TV watching will make you sleepy.) There is something quite invigorating—even exhilarating—about exhausting yourself doing something really, *really* important. When you spend the day being a fully-engaged Strong Happy Mom, you will go to bed with sore feet, a contented smile, and a full heart. You will have spent the day doing something eternally valuable.

Lots of friends my age look back over their parenting careers with deep regrets about opportunities missed. They lament phoning it in as a mom, or jobbing out precious time with their kids. If you're a parent, be a Strong Happy one. Love your kids 'til they can feel it. Correct them when they need it. Listen to them when they bare their souls. Investing your time this way pays dividends that last *forever—literally.*

As a parting note, I'd like to share with you a letter that one of my daughters handed me when we dropped her off at college for the first time. It is rather personal, but with her permission I include it here not because I'm an exhibitionist, but because I want to give you an encouraging glimpse at your potential future.

When you are in the thick of raising children, it is often difficult to know whether the parenting choices you are making will lead to a good end. You reason through various philosophies of parenting, and choose the one that seems wisest, but you're often plagued by doubt and second-guessing. "Ideas have consequences," but you don't get to see the consequences for decades, when it's too late to correct your course. I often wished I had a crystal ball to show me how my parenting strategy would pan out.

Without the help of said crystal ball, with fear and trembling, my husband and I have persevered for over twenty-five years, using the ideas I've described in this book. Some days we were—and still are— complete failures. Now that half of our children are adults, we arc beginning to see the consequences of our ideas. Though none of our kids is perfect (a genetically inherited state, I'm afraid), they have become productive, interesting, thoughtful, funny people. And they all seem grateful for their upbringing.

Here is the closest thing to a crystal ball I can offer you: The attached letter attests, in our daughter's own (slightly hyperbolic) voice, to the strength of ideas by which she was raised. This is not the only letter like this I've received from an adult child—it's just the one that happens to be in my purse right now. I'm not a flawless mom (ask all ten of my kids, and all of my friends), but I hope that perhaps the ideas in this book can give you some help as you build your own Strong Happy Family. And in ten or twenty years, maybe we can sit down for our cup of coffee, and you'll show me the letter your precious child handed you as he left your home. (We better bring tissues.)

Mom,

I can't thank you and Dad enough for the last 19 years. Everything that I am is because of you two.

107

Mom, you are truly the most amazing woman I have ever met. I learn from your example everyday. I don't think you understand how much of a blessing it's been for me to live with this supply of infinite wisdom. Our conversations, your subtle rebukes, your comments that I've rolled my eyes at all have done so much to make me who I am today. You've been teaching me life lessons since I was born and I want you to know how much I appreciate them. I can vividly recall times I thought I'd never talk to you again or that you didn't like me and were purposely making me mad. It's funny then how much I thought I had everything figured out. I want to thank you for being so strong and loving me so much throughout all my tantrums and fights. Thank you for being able to see past my anger, confusion, frustration, and teen angst and know that everything would be OK. Thank you for always wanting what's best for me instead of giving me what I thought was best for me. It's amazing how God has grown and changed our relationship. From changing diapers and cleaning up puke, to Bible studies, to breakdown algebra lessons, to you being my best friend. And the best is yet to come!!!

Some of my friends get a lot of bad advice from their moms; I don't know who I would've become if it weren't for your guidance. Thank you for literally giving me everything! I'm overwhelmed thinking of how you intentionally decided to put all your time, energy and love into this family. You took everything you had and poured it into my life. You are selfless! I know you could do anything you want to, that's why it means so much that you decided to raise up a baby girl (and 9 others.) You have done so much with your life it is AMAZING! Seriously you amaze me by how much you get done. You are the best role model a daughter could ask for, I look up to you more than you'll ever realize. Thanks again for the 19 years at home. Honestly, you and Dad gave me the greatest upbringing possible. God is so good; it's hard to believe I love you so much.

Please call or Skype me whenever you want, I'll be offended if you don't.

Whenever I show an interest in a sport or a topic you always tell me to pursue it. Even if it is probably a silly idea or you know I'll change my mind later on, you let me try it anyway. I hardy ever hear "no" from you, but instead you help me get started and support me along the way.

I can tell you my problems or issues knowing that you trust me. You never pry; you just listen and relieve my stress (because I know you won't say anything). Having you to talk to has made my gossiping almost go away completely. Instead of complaining to my friends, risking having a situation go out of control, I can just tell you in a few short words about my issue and I know you'll understand.

Thank you for trusting me. In high school there is a lot of pressure to do a lot of things and sometimes it gets frustrating. I'm so thankful to have the friends that I do, always encouraging me with their good decisions and having you. For some reason knowing that you trust me to make the right decisions helps me make them. I love the confidence you show me.

I appreciate how you lead by example. As I get older, you no longer tell me how to behave but rather show me. I've grown out of the age of spankings because now I watch you to learn how to act. Your hours of work don't go unnoticed. Oftentimes I'll just stare at you wondering how you still have energy. I know you probably want to scream at me most of the time when you're working and I'm just sitting around but you don't. Instead you just continue to work with a persistently patient attitude toward me that boggles my mind. Without a word you teach me so much! You probably don't agree because after nineteen years with me I'm almost as lazy as I was when you started with me. But really everyday I'm learning and slowly I'm becoming more like you. I know it's a slow process, but it is working.

It's such a blessing being around a woman I respect and enjoy so much.

I love you.